THE GREAT
RADIO
COMEDIANS

By the same author

THE GREAT
RADIO
COMEDIANS

Jim Harmon

DOUBLEDAY & COMPANY, INC., GARDEN CITY, NEW YORK

1970

Publishing Consultant: J. P. Tarcher, Inc.

This book is dedicated to *Jack Benny* for giving me a subject, to *Jeremy Tarcher,* for giving me a chance to write about it, and to my mother, *Valeria Harmon,* for giving me me.

Acknowledgments

My sincere thanks to the following people who helped make this book a reality:

My fellow collectors of the ephemera of the era of radio: Dave Amaral, Dr. Barry Brooks (owner of probably the world's largest radio collection), Ed Corcoran, Dave Dixon of the Canadian Broadcasting Corporation; Morris Scott Dollens, Richard Gulla, Martin Halperin, Chris Lembesis, Lloyd Nesbitt, Professor Lawrence Sharpe of the University of North Carolina, and Johnny Tillotson.

Those who assisted me in preparing material: Kris Neville for the Edgar Bergen sequence; Donald F. Glut for the Bob Hope chapter; Richard Andersen for the Al Jolson sequence; and for general help and advice: Forrest J. Ackerman, Bill Blackbeard, Redd Boggs, Ron Haydock, Paul Kalin, the Reverend Robert E. Neily, Lil Neville, Robert Rosen, Gretchen Schwenn, and Frank E. Swain (the Pulaski, Virginia, police officer whose dedication to the ideas of old time radio earned him an official appointment as the "First Honorary Lone Ranger").

To those dealers in books, magazines, and comics relating to radio and other popular culture who extended to me many personal favors: William Thailing of Cleveland, Ohio; and Burt Blum of the Cherokee Book Store, Hollywood, California.

To those who helped establish that source of recordings and information, *The Jim Harmon Radio Heroes Society, P. O. Box 38612, Hollywood, Calif. 90038.*

To those performers and other creative people from radio: Lee Allman ("Miss Case"), Kirk Alyn ("Superman" of the movie serials, but radio friend of *Portia Faces Life*), Edgar Bergen, Jim Boles ("Doc Long"), Robert Bloch (who wrote for Colonel Stoopnagle before *Psycho*), Jim Conway, Ralph Edwards, Jack Eigen, Shari Lewis, Forrest Lewis ("Wash"), Barbara Luddy, Athena Lord, Charlie McCarthy, Carlton E. Morse, Jay Novello ("Jack Packard"), Tony Randall, Anne Seymour, Lureen Tuttle, George W. Trendle, Olan Soule, and Ezra Stone.

As in *The Great Radio Heroes*, I have no bibliography since most of the books published on radio deal with purely technical electronic matters, or with non-representative prestige presentations (such as Norman Corwin dramas) and not with the actual subject matter of radio broadcasting in the thirties and forties; thus most of my material is from original research by myself. However, two books have been of considerable help to me: *There's Laughter in the Air*, by Jack Gaver and Dave Stanley (Greenberg, 1945), and *Radio's Golden Age*, an index of titles and names compiled by Frank Buxton and Bill Owen (Easton Valley Press, 1966).

Finally, for the over-all concept of this book I wish to thank Ferris Mack of Doubleday, and Jeremy Tarcher and Sy Kasoff of J. P. Tarcher, Inc.

J.H.

Contents

List of Illustrations

following page 76

following page 100

Introduction

Who Did You Listen to Every Sunday?

Everybody listened to the radio on Sunday. Weekdays, kids were going to school, mothers were doing housework, fathers were off doing whatever they did . . . but on Sunday, everybody settled down and listened. A friend of mine tells me his father would turn on the hulking Crosly console on Sunday evenings and say, with a beaming smile: "There's good listening tonight!" There was!

Early on Sunday afternoon there was Gene Autry's *Melody Ranch* (which for my youthful taste had too much singing and comedy with Pat Buttram and too short an adventure story with Gene), and *The Shadow,* who stood for all the mystery and violence in the night we loved so on radio. But more than anything it was Sunday's line-up of comics which turned on the sunshine and laughter: Jack Benny and Fred Allen, and in later years, Eddie Cantor; Amos 'n' Andy, Lum and Abner, and the Phil Harris-Alice Faye show.

(The two worlds of radio, mystery and comedy, met when Jack Benny did a take-off on one of the Shadow's compatriots, the Whistler. "I," intoned Benny, "am the Fiddler and I know many things . . . because I fiddle around a lot.")

No matter who your favorites were during the week, everybody listened to Benny on Sunday, and everybody enjoyed him. Even the kids, like me. Life at that time had not become compartmentalized to the extent it has today. (The next step will be rest rooms marked *MEN, WOMEN,* and *TEEN-AGERS.*) I did not know that Jack Benny was for grown-ups, that Fred Allen was for intellectuals. I liked Jack Benny approximately as much as I liked Jack Armstrong.

If you grew up with radio comedy, you learned to laugh as hard at a pun as at a pratfall. Today you laugh harder at the pseudohostility of Don Rickles because it involves the incisive use of language than you do at the same Rickles being caught up in a live cartoon, getting a bucket of water in his face on *Laugh-In.* Your sense of humor, and the rest of you, has been shaped by a thousand Sundays of hearing Jack Benny satirize the love of money and Fred Allen demolish the standards of bureaucracy.

The great comedians of radio have gone to television, or to semiretirement, or have died. The art of radio comedy lies almost forgotten, like its sister art, radio drama. Radio had its limitations—it was shortest on subtlety. It had its assets— the use of imagination, and the power of suggestion.

The continuing appearance of record albums of audio-only comedy by Bill Cosby, Stan Freberg, Bob Newhart, and others proves that *sound* alone still has its appeal.

As of this writing, Don McNeill has just hung up his coffeepot after over thirty years of getting laughs on the *Breakfast Club* radio show. For three and a half decades, McNeill had marched around the breakfast table, listened to

Sam Cowling telling how he, Sam, was getting so fat he had to order the material for his suits from a carpet show room, and consoled Aunt Fanny when she complained that her friend, Clara, was a terrible gossip, terrible—Clara had told all of Aunt Fanny's friends the latest news before Fanny, herself, could get to them. Now the local stations have won another round in getting more local time for more local commercials. Radio is making more money than ever, but there is no room for the *Breakfast Club.*

There are two network shows still carrying comedy on radio: *Monitor* and Arthur Godfrey.

Godfrey is filling out twenty-five years of his morning show on CBS (although he, personally, goes back in radio nearly forty years). He no longer employs Jan Davis, the Mariners, Tony Marvin, and as is well known, certainly not Julius La-Rosa. They have gone on to other activities, and about Godfrey's only regular is singer Richard Hayes. Arthur still kids his sponsors: "Send in the box-top from Post Bran Flakes for your free coupon. The Post folks need those box-tops. They ran out at the factory, and if they don't get some tops for the boxes, they'll have to send out their flakes loose. And you know those Bran Flake people hate anything loose."

NBC's *Monitor* on Saturdays and Sundays features occasional flashes of comedy. Once in a while, Bob Hope even makes a guest appearance for a few minutes. Jack Benny has been interviewed. And one of the regular hosts or "communicators" is Henry Morgan, certainly one of the outstanding comedians of golden age radio.

Twenty years ago, Morgan was swapping jokes with Fred Allen on his own *Henry Morgan Show.*

ALLEN: I've been listening to your program on the radio, Henry, and you just are not coming over . . . I examined my radio. There was plenty of distilled water in the battery. Both tubes were lit, both aglow. So obviously something is *rotten—* not in my radio, not in Denmark, but right here in this studio . . . Are your jokes fresh and up to date, Henry? Did you tell a Leo Durocher joke, Henry?

MORGAN: Yes, I did . . . I said: "Have you noticed no matter how many times I get fired, Durocher is always one up on me?"

ALLEN: Try me on some other topical gem you must have up your sleeve—its lumpy there, I see . . .

MORGAN: Well, Fred, this fellow was locked in a room for ten years. When he came out, he saw his shadow and went back in . . .

ALLEN: What are your plans for the summer, Henry? What are you replacing yourself with?

Today, on *Monitor,* Morgan still says "Hello anybody—here's Morgan" and introduces a record of low decibel rock 'n' roll —"chicken-rock" to the trade—and then gives a report on the crowning of the Idaho Potato Queen. It is only a weekend diversion from his TV work, but once when he was reading the football game scores of some minor colleges that nobody but the alumni had ever heard of, Morgan suddenly expressed what may be his opinion of the way radio is today: "Is anybody *really* interested in this nonsense?"

To those who are interested in the delightful nonsense that radio used to dispense not so long ago, this book is respectfully submitted.

Jim Harmon
Los Angeles, 1969

THE GREAT
RADIO
COMEDIANS

1.

Those Brats We Loved But Could Never Be

The comedy shows of radio gave the kids who listened to them one vicarious pleasure denied them by the adventure thrillers: an opportunity to get back at their elders. In the afternoon, Jack Armstrong always expressed the utmost respect for his adopted Uncle Jim even when the dottering old fool of forty-some-odd had got them hopelessly trapped in the dungeons of the Crocodile God. "Sir," Jack would aver, "I respect your mature decision that it would have been against your principles to point loaded firearms at those cannibals." But in the evening, we could delight in brash Charlie McCarthy reducing the pedagogical Edgar Bergen to spluttering incoherence. "Bergen—you've already lost your hair! Your teeth may not be around much longer!"

The brats of Radioland were flabbergasting in their contempt for their elders. Every insult, every bit of snideness was clutched to our hearts. Harassed and put upon as we

were by parents, teachers, and any adult who cared to issue
us orders, the wine of insolence was heady indeed. And
grown-ups didn't seem to mind. Perhaps it was all made ac-
ceptable to them by their knowledge that these cheeky and
mouthy brats were in reality adults only pretending to be
children. No child, in real life, would ever talk to his parents
like Red Skelton who played Junior, "The mean widdle kid";
Fanny Brice, ever the classic brat, "Baby Snooks"; and Edgar
Bergen, who was both himself and the voice of his ventriloquist's dummy, Charlie McCarthy.

Of the three, the top-hatted little figure—complete with
monocle, tuxedo, and sassy tongue—gave a more meaningful
visual aid to our fantasies. The image may have been wooden
but it seemed closer to the picture in our imaginations than the
publicity pictures you saw of Skelton or Miss Brice in their
unconvincing childish garb.

Like all the other father figures in radio, Bergen was
thoroughly decent and well-meaning if mildly reproving.
As did Snooks' "Daddy" or Junior's "Mummy," Bergen wanted
the best for his "child," but he apparently didn't understand
that a knowledge of ancient Roman history was of very little
practical use to a boy of ten. Charlie needed to know how to
toss a baseball, or win a fist fight, or perhaps most urgently
he needed some fatherly advice on his favorite subject, girls.
Yet somehow Bergen always missed this point and tried to
fill him with useless, *adult* knowledge.

The humor of the situation sprang from this inevitable
misunderstanding between a rather scholarly man and a high-
school near-dropout with native wit and precocious romantic
interests. What resulted was wildly comic verbal fencing,
perfect for the sound-oriented medium (rather than the conflict of character acted out in a physical situation, as for example, in the *Dennis the Menace* comic strip of today).

Charlie McCarthy knew that the world was his oyster and that the traditional values of Bergen's world were somehow irrelevant to his own problems. It was a gentler generation gap of a less hurried time.

Like much of radio, the word duels between Bergen and McCarthy depended on the logic of the instant. The situation was difficult to sustain plausibly: an intelligent and mature adult forever exasperated by a callow youth. The older generation must have wished at times that Bergen would just say to hell with it and walk away, leaving McCarthy sitting there with his mouth open.

BERGEN: Well I can see, Charlie, that I'll have to give you a simple illustration of how the brain works.
CHARLIE: Yes, sir, and you've got the brain that can do it.
BERGEN: I say to myself—
CHARLIE: Oh, do you?
BERGEN: I want to move my left arm—see. And it moves.
CHARLIE: By golly, it did, didn't it! Oh, you're so clever. Do you tie your own shoelaces too?

Exasperating to some adults, but we who were children at the time loved it. Oh, if we could only top our instructors at home and at school with such infuriating superiority. . . .

Though radio seemed to realize the lure buried in our unconscious of the adult being able to return to the sense of wonder of being a child again, nobody in radio was aware of how attractive it might be to a child to become an adult. Only the comic books, the other great source of escape for children in the forties, gave us the story of *Captain Marvel* in which young (twelve-year-old, perhaps) Billy Batson could change to the World's Mightiest Man by saying the magic word, "Shazam!" Captain Marvel never made it to radio. His rival, *Superman,* did, but when actor Bud Collyer changed from the mild-manner tenor of Clark Kent to the forceful bass of Superman, he only changed his working clothes from a business suit to red-and-blue cape and tights. Both sides of Superman's personality were relentlessly serious and adult.

Billy Batson and Charlie McCarthy had certain similarities. Neither in their less-than-adult identities was actually as powerless against the forces of the adult world as were real youngsters. Even in his boy identity, Billy Batson was a famous radio reporter with privileges to ride fire trucks and visit the scenes of celebrated ax murders. Charlie McCarthy may have been stuck with school work, but he did it wearing a tuxedo and monocle. Charlie visited nightclubs and he flirted outrageously with Lana Turner. Both were better off than their listeners, by a damsite, but neither were ever begrudged their unique place in the course of things.

I can visualize Charlie McCarthy and Billy Batson meeting each other for the first time. It would probably be in the backroom of some nightclub. Charlie has just come in to look for an unstoppered decanter. Billy is there to look through the papers of the club's owner, a notorious gangster.

"Holy Moley!" Billy exclaims. "What's a kid like you doing in a tough hangout like this?"

"Aw, shutup, or I'll blow you down," McCarthy responds not unkindly.

"Look, you could get into a lot of trouble if Bugbrain McGurkle comes in here," Billy tells Charlie.

"I might get into a lot of trouble if Jane Russell comes in," Charlie goes on, with a wink. "That's what I'm waiting for."

"Believe me," Billy says earnestly, "I'm telling you for your own good to get out of here. I know what I'm talking about. You see, I have the wisdom of Solomon."

"Funny," says Charlie, "you don't look Jewish."

"I also have the strength of Hercules. I use that when the wisdom of Solomon fails."

"Why, you little shrimp," blusters Charlie, "if you try to strongarm me, I'll call Edgar Bergen."

"And if you don't leave," Billy says with youthful maturity, "I'll call Captain Marvel."

"I just came in to find a Kleenex to swob a speck of sawdust from my monocle," Charlie says with typical discretion. "I'll be gone before you can say 'Shalom.'"

"Shazam," Billy corrects him, and Charlie dashes out as the magic lightning flashes down.

Charlie McCarthy's character of brashness, irreverence, and toothless threats was well known to every radio listener. He became a real person to most of us. Few people ever said, "Let's listen to Edgar Bergen." Hardly more said, "Let's tune in Bergen and McCarthy." Most of us said, "Let's listen to Charlie McCarthy."

The wooden dummy captured the fascination of a public harried by the threat of war, humbled by the continuing depression. He was pampered more than many humans. He drew on wooden organ banks for replacement of limbs and torso through the years, but the original head, repainted and repaired as necessary, remains to this writing the same as it was in the beginning, almost half a century ago. As time wore on, it seemed that Charlie McCarthy achieved the ambition of the puppet, Pinocchio, and turned into a real boy. For one of the several Bergen and McCarthy movies, it was announced that Charlie McCarthy would even now be able to walk.

If, unlike Pinocchio, Charlie never became flesh and blood,

he earned what Pinocchio *really* sought: although only wood
and imagination, Charlie captured the *love* of his creator and
a host of friends that included most of the American public.

The dummy came so much alive that it suppressed the
man, Bergen, in the public view, as it was meant to do. It
was only natural to wonder how the creator of Charlie Mc-
Carthy felt about the little top-hatted figure. Had he developed the same emotional attachment to the wooden dummy
and the disembodied voice that we had? All of us, as girls
and boys, weave fantasies with baby dolls and toy soldiers
which become very real. Was it true for Edgar Bergen himself?

In 1937, Bergen drew up a will leaving McCarthy ten
thousand dollars.

> I, Edgar John Bergen, give and bequeath to the Actors' Fund
> of America the sum of Ten Thousand dollars to be . . . used . . .
> to give gratuitous and charitable performances of ventriloquism
> . . . at orphanages, welfare homes, homes for crippled children
> . . . "Charlie McCarthy" the dummy, has been my constant
> companion and has taken on the character of a real person and
> from whom I have never been separated for even a day . . .
> Ventriloquists so selected . . . shall always use "Charlie
> McCarthy" when giving such . . . performances . . .

In March 1939, the heir to this small fortune, like many
another wealthy child of the depression, was *kidnapped*. The
nation was so upset that the Federal Bureau of Investigation
was called in on the case. It turned out to be the practical
joke of a newspaperman friend, and after about twenty-four
hours, Charlie was back home. His harried master was established to be completely innocent of any involvement.

Edgar Bergen was a senior in high school when he first

sketched the face of Charlie McCarthy on the flyleaf of his history book. His model was a street urchin newsboy Bergen had once known. A popular story has it that the wood-carver's knife slipped, giving Charlie a peculiar slanted expression in one eye. However, like so many legends, the man whom the legend concerns knows nothing about the story. "Charlie looked fine to me right from the beginning," Bergen told this writer recently. Charlie was the first dummy of his own. He did not need to experiment further.

As a boy, he had been proficient in "throwing his voice" and tricking friends into thinking someone was outside the door. (Bergen's own voice was touched with the vaguely exotic aura of his Swedish ancestry, although he is an American, born in Chicago on February 16, 1903.) Although he had what seemed to be mystical control over his voice, when his gifts became the object of national curiosity, he avoided making extravagant claims regarding his ability and expressed doubts that the voice could actually be thrown. Indeed, there was something eerie about it, and the listener—as in watching stage magic—found himself wanting to believe that there was, in spite of denials, real magic involved.

The question of the division of identity always arises in connection with a ventriloquist. Does Edgar Bergen really think of Charlie McCarthy as a separate person? The answer is not entirely clear. "A comedian like Bob Hope or Charlie can get away with saying things I can't," Bergen said recently. "Sometimes I wish I could walk into a room and be as readily accepted as Charlie." Is he then jealous of Charlie? "I don't care which of us they like the better." Then he never feels any hostility toward Charlie? "Only when he says something I don't expect him to say."

Edgar Bergen has always felt, however, that he and Char-

lie McCarthy have much in common. Bergen's own background was middle class and not on the destitution level of
the urchin after whom he named Charlie, but he knew as
many thorns as roses. Working as a paid performer with
Charlie, he got through high school, and went on to North-
western University, where his original ambition to become a
physician was progressively corroded by successes in local
theaters. Transferring to a speech course, he obtained his degree by going to summer sessions, working the winter months
in vaudeville.

Bergen spent ten years on the fading vaudeville circuit,
performing what was never regarded as more than a standard
ventriloquist act. He visited Europe and Russia and South
America and gradually refined and polished the personality
of McCarthy. The newsboy figure became clothed in a tiny
tuxedo and developed a worldly accent learned in his travels.
There was now a peculiarly electric tension in the small voice
with a trace of a British accent that contrasted nicely with
the soft Scandinavian tones of Bergen.

Late in 1936, Bergen made a guest appearance on *The
Rudy Vallee Show.* The singer-comedian predicted that these
two people—"No, only one," he corrected himself—would go
far. And he was right. They were a hit. In a comparatively
short time, Bergen and McCarthy were starring on *The Chase
and Sanborn Hour,* earning two hundred thousand dollars a
year, a hundred thousand dollars apiece!

The weekly show featured a cast of regulars seldom
equaled even in radio where the supporting performers
tended to be stronger than in television. Ray Noble led a
bright, swinging orchestra and in addition was a fine light
English comedian. "We liked to give Ray parts in sketches
like that of a Southern colonel," Bergen recalled. The singer

on the show was the famous opera star Nelson Eddy. "Nelson had led a rather sheltered life, and he never seemed to be able to unbend enough to tell a joke. We made a joke out of the fact that every time Nelson tried to tell a funny story, it fell flat." The master of ceremonies was Don Ameche (before he invented the telephone) and, according to Bergen, "one of the cleverest ad libbers I have ever worked with."

The permanent guest star on the show for some time was the fabulous W. C. Fields. "Fields was the most talented man I ever worked with anywhere," Bergen recalled. "He could read a joke somebody wrote for him. He could write his own joke and deliver it masterfully. And he was a master of pantomime—which had no part in radio, of course, except for the occasional benefit of our studio audience."

Fields is regarded by many film critics as being in a league with Charlie Chaplin for the title of World's Greatest Comedian. His radio work was minor compared to his film classics like *The Bank Dick, You Can't Cheat an Honest Man,* and *Never Give a Sucker an Even Break,* but even in standardized exchanges between himself and Charlie Mc-Carthy, Fields managed to project his unique comic genius.

The most frequent image of Fields in radio or movies was that of a drunk. Yet Fields was seldom if ever drunk. In fact, he despised the slobbering, incoherent, wobbling state of drunkenness in himself and in others. Guests at his house who thought it was expected of them to get as besotted as Fields was alleged to get were seldom invited back. He was a man of precision and balance in his speech and in his body movements.

"Bill Fields would show up in the morning at rehearsals with his Thermos bottle of martinis," Bergen remembered. "He would be drinking in the morning, drinking at noon, drinking in the afternoon. But he *never* acted as if he were drunk." In forty years of doing a juggling act in vaudeville, appearing in Broadway shows like the *Ziegfeld Follies,* and performing comedy on screen and radio, he never missed a performance.

W. C. Fields' first venture into radio came in a special broadcast honoring film pioneer Adolphe Zukor. The great comedian was recuperating in a sanitarium at the time—his use of alcohol may have been largely medicinal but it was nonetheless hard on his liver. Fields broadcast his portion of the show from his hospital room, and although weak of body, his voice came across strong and with its usual asperity.

Radio work beckoned as a source of employment that offered less physical exertion than motion pictures while he regained his strength. In 1937 Fields appeared on *The Chase and Sanborn Hour,* starring Edgar Bergen and Charlie McCarthy. It was chance casting, but it worked admirably, and Fields stayed with the show as a regular until the summer of 1939. Though Charlie McCarthy was a child, his character was much like that of Fields'. Both were street urchins who had never fully grown up. Both were irreverent and cynical on the surface, with an underlying sentimentality. Of course, for the purposes of comedy, there had to be more than similarity—there had to be conflict. It stemmed from the fact that Charlie McCarthy *was* a child, one made of wood and Bergen's voice, but still a child. And, happily, Fields couldn't stand children.

His dislike of children was genuine—great psychological insight is not needed to see that he envied their good fortune in not having to endure the miserable horror he had known as a child. Though he and Bergen were friends, Fields thought of Charlie as a separate, living human being, and on a few occasions, Bergen actually had to restrain Fields from damaging the valuable dummy in a fit of rage.

Before Charlie came out of his case, Fields was pliable enough. He and Bergen would sit around "dirtying up the script"—which Bergen hastens to explain meant they wrote all over it in pencil, adding lines in order to top the other. Even these changes were not enough for Fields, and he frequently did considerable "rewriting" on the air. While not the comic genius Fields was, Bergen did manage to follow the wild directions Bill Fields sometimes took, as in the following unscripted change:

FIELDS: To be perfectly frank with you, Edgar, I've never trusted either of you.

CHARLIE: What do you mean by that crack? I want you to know that Bergen is just as honest as you, you crook, you.

FIELDS: That tips off the whole thing. You'd better come out of the sun, Charles, before you get unglued.

CHARLIE: Do you mind if I stand in the shade of your nose?

FIELDS: Quiet, you termite flophouse.

Most of the verbal duels between Fields and McCarthy followed a set pattern. Occasionally, for variety, bandleader Ray Noble or master of ceremonies Don Ameche would be introduced into the conversation.

DON: You shouldn't always be fighting with Charlie, Bill . . .

FIELDS: You're talking to a new Fields, Don . . . I'm full of the spirit of friendship . . . every night . . .

CHARLIE: Here I am, Mr. Fields.

FIELDS: Well, well, Charlie McCarthy, my little pal. I've missed you. Been carrying the torch for you.

CHARLIE: I can see it on your nose.

FIELDS: Bright little nipper. That a new paint job he has there, Edgar?

CHARLIE: If I had a wick on me, I'd stick it in your mouth and rent you out as an alcohol lamp.

DON: Charlie, Charlie, Bill didn't come here to argue. He's a new Fields.

CHARLIE: So I've got new Fields to conquer . . .

FIELDS: Is it true your father was a gate-leg table?

CHARLIE: If it is, your father was under it!

Don Ameche recalled recently that among the weekly guest stars on *The Chase and Sanborn Hour* was Mae West. Like Fields, Miss West managed to make everything she said sound suggestive. Fields' oath of "Godfrey Daniel!" always came across as "Goddam!" Even when Mae said something like, "Let's go to church next Sunday," it would come out as a very intimate invitation. Again like Bill Fields, Mae West wrote much of her own material. For her appearance on one show, she wrote a play about Adam and Eve.

Ameche watched the rehearsals with growing alarm. The lines might have been innocent enough, but Mae West's delivery was not. Finally, Ameche concluded that all of their jobs were in jeopardy and tried to get the producer and then Bergen to drop the sketch from the show.

This show included such lines as Mae West, as Eve, saying, "You've got to stop laying around loafing, Adam. It's time to turn over a new leaf." Then Adam would say, "I don't care a fig if I do." The mail that poured in caused Mae West to be barred from radio, allegedly "for life" (although she did some shows in the fifties) and caused serious trouble for the rest of the cast and crew.

W. C. Fields probably enjoyed the uproar hugely. He had enough of his own troubles with sponsors.

When Fields finally graduated from the Chase and San-

born show to do a short-lived series of his own, he made
numerous droll references to his son, Chester. It is doubtful
if his sponsors, Lucky Strike cigarettes, ever could do anything about Fields' wicked play-on-words.

A man of monumental pettiness and eccentricity, with a
hundred categories of hatreds and dislikes, W. C. Fields remained, beneath it all, a street urchin in long pants, only a
tall brat, attacking the petty meannesses of a world that had
hurt him.

Edgar Bergen was left with only a smaller brat, Charlie.
Charlie was perfect but who among us is content with mere
perfection? With much fanfare and anticipation, Bergen introduced a second dummy in 1938. It was Mortimer Snerd,
the total country bumpkin. Mortimer's denseness made for
a dialogue full of leisurely repetition, hardly suited, it would
seem, to the fast pace of radio comedy. But the appeal of the
hick, the person who is even dumber than we are, has
proved timeless. A typical exchange between Mortimer and
guest star Jane Powell would go like this.

JANE: Morty, what does spring mean to you?
MORTIMER: Spring? Well, spring means I can take my long
    underwear off.
BERGEN: No, no, certainly not!
MORTIMER: Leave 'em on?
BERGEN: Mortimer, how can you be so stupid?
MORTIMER: It's clean living that did it.

Today, Edgar Bergen still continues to appear with Charlie
McCarthy on occasional television programs. But as Charlie
Chaplin has observed, when a man—even a man who is a
comedian—grows older, he longs for something with a bit
more dignity. Bergen has for some years played many interesting character roles in movies, and must of his interest

lies in this area—creating new characters, especially through the use of make-up, a neglected art among modern comedians.

Still, Charlie McCarthy is never very far from Edgar Bergen. Sometime back, they did a series of one-minute radio commercials. Did he actually bring the dummy into the radio studios that had not seen an audience in decades? Edgar Bergen was genuinely astounded. "How could Charlie be there if—Charlie wasn't there?" he asked. "My timing would be off," he amended.

Of course Charlie was there. The question really didn't have to be asked.

THAT MEAN WIDDLE KID

The small boy that is forever a part of Red Skelton was known as "Junior, the mean widdle kid." He was a little red-headed tyke who, when confronted with the temptation to do mischief, *always* gave in—after a transparently insincere hesitation—with the whooping cry, "I dood it." No cookie jar was safe from breaking, no grown-up free from outrageous needling. In fact, Junior would be in such a hurry to needle visiting neighbor (and show announcer) Rod O'Connor that he'd slide down the banister and land with a thump! at the bottom of the stairs.

JUNIOR: Oh, I hit me crazy bone, I hit me crazy bone!
MOTHER: Well, if you comb your hair right, it won't show . . .
    I'm sorry, Junior. I've been nursing a grouch all day.
JUNIOR: Do tell! Pop sick?
    (*Knock at door.*)
O'CONNOR: Hello, hello, hello!
JUNIOR: Awwww, *shut up!* You big fat blimp!

O'CONNOR: Junior, why do you call me a big fat blimp?
JUNIOR: I calls them the way I sees 'em.
O'CONNOR: You know . . . I painted my new fence white. Now my black car has white fingerprints on it.
JUNIOR: Goodness me, the phantom has struck again!

Like many modern children, Junior passed through the guardianship of a number of parents. His original mother was Harriet Hilliard who was primarily the girl singer with Ozzie Nelson's band on the show. Later, Ozzie and Harriet moved over to a show of their own, detailing for many years their family life as husband and wife on both radio and television. David Rose's orchestra took up residence on the Skelton show, and Junior got a new mom—the much-traveled Lureen Tuttle. At another period, he was in the custody of his grandmother, "Nanmaw" Verna Felton. The changing family scene occurred frequently in radio but apparently had little effect on Junior. Nor was his sense of security much impaired by frequent suggestions from an exasperated parent that he go outside and play, or by them *daring* him to hold his breath until he turned blue.

Skelton had been a small boy in real life once, of course. He was born in Vincennes, Indiana, in 1913, and went through an unusual series of jobs before he was out of his teens: newsboy, poolroom assistant, pitchman with a traveling patent medicine show, showboat and minstrel troup entertainer. Finally, he got to work in a theater that stood still in one spot—a burlesque house. More legitimate shows on Broadway followed, and the young comic got a small but memorable part as the social director at Camp Carefree in the movie, *Having Wonderful Time*. A radio show followed, interrupted by Army service in World War II. Since then, Skelton has never missed a season on radio or TV. His first wife, Edna

Stillwell, was a talented comedy writer and helped him develop, with her insight into Skelton's own personality, many of his classic characterizations. (In his postwar movie, *The Fuller Brush Man*, Skelton's most popular role was made visual for the first time. "Junior" was played by a real little boy hired for the movie, while the grownup Skelton played straight man. The comedian went through a routine in which he heard his own radio lines fed back to him by the boy and suffered through being constantly topped by the ghost of himself! Later, the problem of making Junior visual on television was solved with only partial success by having Red appear in giant-sized short pants.) Fortunately, Skelton had many other characters he could pull out of himself. Though they were adult in nature, the mischievous Junior lurked behind each.

Some weeks, Skelton would appear as Deadeye, a somewhat disreputable Western character. Deadeye would enter in a cloud of dust, crying "Whoa—whoa—come on horse, *whoooa!*" Finally, in desperation, he would shoot his unfortunate mount *dead*—the only way this slightly daffy cowboy could get his horse to stop.

Sauntering nonchalantly into the saloon, Deadeye would down some redeye, and ogle the dancehall girls with his good orb. Always, always, some cowhand would take offense to him and call for a shoot out. That was keeno with Deadeye. They would shoot on the count of three, Deadeye ordered.

DEADEYE: One . . . Two . . .
   (*Sound: gunshot bangs.*)
DEADEYE: Three!

They never seemed to learn. Finally, Deadeye picked a fight with a particularly desperate character. Deadeye began counting: "One!" he said. *Bang!* went the gunshot, and *Deadeye* toppled to the floor. "Why did you do a low, underhanded thing like that, Stranger?" Deadeye gasped. "I've heard this show before," the stranger declared.

If Deadeye was an anticipation of the anti-hero popular in modern Westerns, Red Skelton also carried on the tradition of country bumpkin humor so popular on television. He was Clem Kadiddlehopper, who was always absolutely astonished to see his girl friend: *"Weeell—Daisy June!"*

Clem's open-mouthed innocence had much the same quality as Mortimer Snerd's. Apparently in both Edgar Bergen and in Red Skelton, and perhaps in all of us, there lies a secret self that feels ignorant in the face of the mysteries and complexities of the world.

As for Daisy June, who was always greeted so energetically, she must have been doomed by fate to troublesome males in her life. Actress Lureen Tuttle was not only Clem's girl friend, Daisy June, but the "mean widdle kid's" mother, as well. She couldn't win.

Miss Tuttle was also occasionally foil to other Skelton characterizations, such as Willy Lump-Lump, a slightly punch-drunk tramp, and J. Newton Numbskull, a typically henpecked husband. The basic character of Red Skelton was subcutaneously underlaid in each. All had a certain sense of wonder about them. Clem expressed this when his girl friend—who like Li'l Abner's Daisy Mae, always seemed to have trouble getting him into a romantic mood—commented on the sounds of a rural night.

DAISY JUNE: Listen to them June bugs all snuggled down cozy in the grass, chirping away, Clem. Why can't we do something like that?

CLEM: Shucks, Daisy June, I can't rub my hind legs together to chirp like them bugs.

Clem said it, but the remark reflected much the same not-quite-of-this-world attitude as that of the classic Skelton comedy character, Junior, the "mean widdle kid."

"FUNNY GIRL"

The magic of radio enabled many performers to extend careers that seemed ended in other media. Considerably past middle age, Fanny Brice's career on stage and on screen was in decline when she first went into radio. She had been a *Ziegfeld Follies* star on Broadway from 1910 through 1923, after the usual climb up through small theaters and the chorus line. She did all sorts of skits and all sorts of songs from the dialect *Rose of Washington Square* to the plaintive romantic *My Man*. One sketch she did, written especially for her by Moss Hart, concerned a mischievous child known as Baby Snooks. She brought this character to radio on a show called *Good News of 1938,* and she played virtually nothing but this character on various radio shows for the rest of her life.

Snooks was the typical comedy child of radio, showing the same irreverence for institutions expressed by Charlie McCarthy and Skelton's "Junior." The audience could take out its own hostility on the world vicariously, without feeling seriously threatened. These deflations of adult Americans were after all, the mere drooling, insinuating prattlings of a child. It was a one-note characterization for a fine comedienne, but nevertheless, Miss Brice probably emerges as the leading solo female comic of radio.

Snooks' long put-upon "Daddy," Lancelot Higgins, was in real life actor Hanley Stafford. He always tried to be calm and reasonable, a loving parent, in dealing with a preambulating package of nitroglycerin. (If Stafford was always on the receiving end as "Daddy," he showed he could dish it out, too, when on another night each week he played J. C. Dithers, the boss of *Blondie's* husband, Dagwood. Stafford joined film players Penny Singleton and Arthur Lake in the comic strip adaptation, thus being co-star of *two* of the very top-rated comedy shows of radio.)

Along with a cast that included fast-talking Arline Harris as Snooks' mother, Stafford and Miss Brice painted a cozy picture each week of a typical American home dominated by a small rampaging demon.

Snooks' schemes were as endless as her decades long childhood. She was capable of putting a bee's nest under the tea cozy at her mother's club meeting. She had no hesitation about cutting her father's fishing line into foot-long bits and rewinding it, ready for fly casting. A more ambitious scheme called for cutting the fur off her mother's mink coat, pasting it all over her baby brother Robespierre and selling him to a neighborhood boy for fifty cents as a pet monkey.

It is no wonder that at one time "Daddy" tried to enroll Snooks in a school for very "exceptional" children.

SNOOKS: Daddy . . .

DADDY: What?

SNOOKS: Is this Miss Gooseberry's school?

DADDY: Snooks, the lady's name is not Gooseberry. It's Shrewsbury, and they want you to be very careful while you're inside. Miss Shrewsbury doesn't admit every little girl. There are one hundred and ten students in her private school.

SNOOKS: That ain't so private.

DADDY: Snooks, we speak of a private school as opposed to a public school, which admits anyone. A public school has a large body of students. Miss Shrewsbury has a small body.

SNOOKS: Is she a midget?
DADDY: No, she happens to be a very cultured and dignified
lady.
SNOOKS: Who?
DADDY: Who have we been talking about?
SNOOKS: Miss Gooseberry.
DADDY: *Shrewsbury!*

Although he was too old to court her, Snooks' gentleman
friend of many years was Frank Morgan, Hollywood's spluttering master of the tall tale and the unexpected Spoonerism.
A typical Morgan story might involve his buying the biggest
sheep ranch in Australia where all the young sheep were
dyed appropriate colors *before* being sheared for the sweater
factory. "Yes, Jockey," Morgan said, as he did in referring to
whoever played his straight man, "that was how I became
known as one of the biggest lamb dyers in the world."

Frank Morgan and Miss Brice as Baby Snooks shared
a show together for a decade (although appearing in entirely
separate acts), but eventually Morgan went to a show featuring himself along with Don Ameche and Frances Langford
called appropriately *The Morgan-Ameche-Langford Show.*
(One sketch that Ameche and Langford did about a quarrel-
some couple known as *The Bickersons* had a long life of its
own and still turns up in radio commercials.) After Morgan's
departure, Baby Snooks finally succeeded in graduating, not
from grade school, but to her own half-hour show.

Fanny Brice differed from all the other comediennes of
radio since, as Snooks, she was more interested in taking
candy from a baby—her brother, Robespierre, to be exact—
than in landing a beau. All the other female comics doing
a solo act were obsessed with the opposite sex. Joan Davis,
Judy Canova, Eve Arden as herself and later as *Our Miss*

Brooks, all seemed mad to get a man. Compare the bawling pest that was Baby Snooks with the incessant man-chasing of Joan Davis.

JOAN: Did you just get in town, Cowboy?
COWBOY: Yep!
JOAN: Do you know any girls in town?
COWBOY: Nope!
JOAN: Would you like to go out with a girl?
COWBOY: Yep!
JOAN: Would you like to go out with me?
COWBOY: Nope!
JOAN: Why, pardner, how can you stand there and say that to me? Me, Gower Gulch Gertie!
COWBOY: But, ma'am, you don't look like you've ever been on a horse.
JOAN: Never been on a horse? Look again, pardner—I didn't get these yere bow-legs from ridin' a pickle barrel!

There was less of the alter-ego aspect to Brice and Snooks than there was to Red Skelton and Junior, and Edgar Bergen and Charlie McCarthy. On her earlier broadcasts, Fanny Brice did at times appear as herself and sing one of her famous songs in her own voice. But in later years, she appeared only as Snooks. There were millions of Americans who had scarcely heard of the *Ziegfeld Follies,* much less having seen it. (It is a curiously provincial thought-pattern of New York City dwellers to assume that anything that ever happened in New York is known to the whole nation and is of interest to that nation.) Many listeners began to accept Snooks as a real child. I recall thinking cannily as a small boy that she was probably really a teen-ager. Fanny Brice's real self was not so much subjugated to Snooks as completely absorbed by the character.

Baby Snooks, Junior, Charlie McCarthy—oh, if we could only get away with some of the things they did as a matter of course. They remain, always, those wonderful brats of radio we loved but could never be.

2.

Wistful Vista

The most practiced liar in Radioland, Fibber McGee, would inevitably have for his best friend the most pompous windbag on the air, Throckmorton P. Gildersleeve. They were the foremost of many citizens on a street called Wistful Vista. (The name seems even more appropriate in retrospect than it did at the time.) Every Tuesday evening during the colder months of the thirties and forties these two cronies got together with a group of other colorful suburbanites. The hostess was the Fibber's wife, Molly.

Fibber McGee and Molly was one of three outstanding comedy shows on NBC Tuesday nights. Unlike Bob Hope and Red Skelton, whose format was made up of separate segments—chitchat with guest stars, a musical number or two, and several comedy sketches—Fibber and Molly presented a show that was all of a piece: you did not have to change your visualization of the setting every few minutes.

The scene was virtually always the McGees' living room into which dropped the same guests every week. This was the era of the dance band remotes from the Avalon Ballroom in Chicago with Wayne King and from the Roosevelt Hotel in New York with Guy Lombardo. Like those shows, you could easily imagine you were listening to a comedy remote from the McGees' living room at 79 Wistful Vista.

The setting, itself, was the typical American living room, and, in fact, you never had much occasion to go into the McGees' kitchen or dining room, certainly not the bedroom. The only other door ever opened besides the front door was the one to the hall closet. Behind it was hidden the accumulated memorabilia of most American families, opening on a million past mistakes—bladeless can openers, never-used skis, long-discarded mandolins. Out it all came in a shameless cascade—*BAM! POW! THUD! SMASH! KER-R-R-RASH! Tinkle. Ting!* It was an auditory pop-art experience.

"Got to clean that hall closet one of these days," Fibber McGee would muse with complacent good intentions. He never did, of course. He never even remembered not to open that door again once he got all the junk piled back precariously inside.

When the program first went on the air, Fibber was a compulsive daydreamer and liar, and his tall tales lacked charm. He was not someone to whom the audience could relate and the series had a limited potential. However his character began to mellow in less than a year and soon he was doing no more impractical dreaming than the rest of us—that is, still quite a lot. And like the rest of us, Fibber had someone to hold him down closer to reality—the little woman, Molly.

Molly was the practical one of the family, somewhat comparable to Belle, the wife of crackpot inventor Lorenzo

Jones on that other radio serial. But Molly was a bit more fun than Belle. Her Irish brogue was laced with Gaelic wit and she was capable of advising Fibber that his latest scheme was no more practical than a square egg; that it was as original as spreading butter on bread; that it stood to make them as much money as selling subscriptions to a censored edition of the *National Geographic*. But in spite of it all, Molly stood dutifully by and tried to help her husband through whatever nonsense he was up to that week.

In private life, Fibber McGee and Molly were actually a married couple, Jim and Marion Jordan. They had met shortly before World War I at a choir rehearsal at St. John's Church in Peoria, Illinois. They both loved music; in fact, while Jim worked as a hardware clerk, Marion Driscoll taught piano lessons. Jim's ambition to be a singer complemented hers and they talked of doing a vaudeville act together. Meanwhile, as a singer, Jim was having a spot of success as a tenor in an act called *A Night with the Poets*. The pay was good for the times—that is, not quite good enough to actually eat on. Jim Jordan returned to Peoria and got a job as a mailman. With some sense of security now, he asked Marion to marry him.

They married in 1918—not a good year for unruffled domestic bliss. After several attempts to enlist, Jim Jordan was called up on a draft quota and was sent to France. Influenza put him on his back in the hospital, while the likes of Sergeant Alvin York and Eddie Rickenbacker and (according to the pulp magazines) *G-8 and his Battle Aces* did the actual fighting. Afterward, Jordan did a man-killing round of appearances as an entertainer for the troops still left in Europe.

When he got back, Jim and Marion spent the next several years going between mundane jobs and vaudeville appearances, while raising two small children. They got their first radio work singing commercials on WJBO in 1925. In 1927, they began doing *The Smith Family,* a sort of white man's *Amos 'n' Andy* on WENR Chicago.

It was 1931 before they got together with Don Quinn, a one-time cartoonist turned radio script writer. Their first series together was called *Smackouts,* about a talkative grocer who was always "smackout" of everything. It was a mixed success, but it drew the attention of John J. Lewis, an important advertising agency representative, and he helped the trio get a network show. It was for this show that Don Quinn created the characters, Fibber McGee and Molly. Success in radio and in several Hollywood films soon followed.

Oddly enough, the way Jim and Marion Jordan met, fell in love, got married, and went into show business seems almost exactly right for the fictional characters of Fibber McGee and Molly. Didn't they both often talk of the old days in Peoria? Didn't he sometimes get his mandolin from that accursed hall closet and plunk away on a few tunes to prove that he had once been a big star on the vaudeville circuit? Jim and Marion Jordan were not *exactly* identical to Fibber McGee and Molly, but the line that separated them was thin and wavering.

It was Don Quinn who molded the Jordans into the McGees with his masterful scripts. Like Paul Rhymer, who wrote *Vic and Sade,* he dealt with middle class, Midwestern types. Unlike Rhymer, he painted with broad strokes and easy exaggerations, creating catch-phrases for his characters that soon became part of the language. Both men, in the opinion of many critics, such as James Thurber, Goodman Ace, and Alexander Woollcott, were on a plane comparable to writers such as Damon Runyon and Ring Lardner, who wrote in a less-perishable medium.

Given the characters of Fibber McGee and Molly in their own closet-dominated home, all that was needed to start off one of their Tuesday night shows was the tiniest of premises. Fibber might be looking through the old photo album of all their dear old friends in Peoria—"There's Fred Lompac—we were together all through high school—never could stand him." Or Molly might be trying to get Fibber to gather up their forest of empty milk bottles and take them in for 2¢ on the bottle. Or on any number of occasions, they might be cleaning up the disaster left by opening that hall closet door.

FIBBER: Gotta straighten out that closet one of these days, Molly. I don't see that electric cord anyplace . . . Oh, my gosh!

MOLLY: Now what?

FIBBER: Look! My old mandolin—remember?

MOLLY: What are you getting so misty eyed about it now for? It falls out of the closet every time you open it.

FIBBER: It always falls out of the closet but this is the first time the case has busted open. My gosh—my old mandolin.
(*Plunks a tune.*)
Needs a little tuning, I guess.

MOLLY: A little tuning! That's as melodious as a slate pencil!

FIBBER: Remember how we used to go canoeing on the Illinois River and I used to serenade you . . . ?

MOLLY: I never knew whether you took up the mandolin because you loved music or hated paddling.

FIBBER: And remember the time you dropped the paddle to applaud one of my songs and we had to paddle home with the mandolin?

MOLLY: I wasn't applauding. I was swatting mosquitoes.

Somehow, the McGees never managed to spend a quiet Tuesday evening at home alone. There was always a parade of guests dropping in, a sort of "Allen's Alley" in reverse. One of their guests in later years was Doctor Gamble, a medico who was vastly more intelligent, if not always more clever, then McGee. Fibber would dazzle him with another of his trademarks: stupefying eliteration.

GAMBLE: Hello, Molly. Hiya, Neanderthal.

FIBBER: Hiya, Arrowsmith. Kick your case of corn cures into a corner and compose your corpulent corpus on a convenient camp chair.

GAMBLE: Thanks, McGee. Your hospitality is equaled only by your personal beauty . . .

MOLLY: Had a lot of operations, Doctor? You look tired.

GAMBLE: My dear, I've had more people in stitches today than Bob Hope. But tell me, what's our one-string fiddler doing with the pot-bellied Strativarius?

FIBBER: This, my ignorant bone-bender, is a mandolin. . . .

GAMBLE: If you really get good with that syncopating cigar box, McGee, and want to run away and join the gypsies, I'll be glad to pierce your ears for earrings . . .

FIBBER: . . . When did you become a music critic, you big fat epidemic chaser?

GAMBLE: Why, you uncultured little faker, I've got more music in the first phalanx of my left pinkie than you have in your whole family tree!

FIBBER: Don't call me a phalanx, you soggy, sap-headed serum salesman!

The conflict between Doctor Gamble and McGee was allegedly good humored, although I've come within a whisker of being punched in the jaw for less. This rivalry was typical of that between McGee and a number of his guests, including not only Gamble (played by Arthur Q. Bryan) but Gale Gordon as Mayor LaTrivia, who was a well-meaning vote-solicitor but who McGee and even a mischievous Molly always tricked into some exasperating tongue twister. "Why, yes, Mrs. McGee, I suppose you would call the minister who sells gasoline in Peoria as a sideline a part-harm, petrol-packing possum—that is, a part-time, pistol-peddling parson—I MEAN, A POT-FARMED POSSUM-PINKING PARTRIDGE!!! Oooooh, *good day!*"

A more restrained rivalry was present between McGee and the Old Timer. Fibber would launch into a new joke he had heard about a man who had cut himself a toupée from his wife's mink stole and was promptly attacked on the street by a rabbit-hunting dog. "That's pretty good, Johnny," the Old Timer would wheeze, "but that ain't the way I heerd it. One feller sez to the other feller, he sez— 'Say, I see you sprouted a new head of hair over night.' The other feller replies 'Over night? I had to pay the store on this for six months!'"

The Old Timer was played by Bill Thompson, who changed his voice to milksop level and became that other visitor at 79 Wistful Vista, Wallace Whimple, who never argued with anyone. His weekly complaint was always about his "big, old fat wife, Sweetieface." Clearly, he got all the action he needed at home. Occasionally even the worm would rotate slightly. "Sweetieface complained that the gelatin dessert I made for her wasn't firm enough. So I mixed cement into it." Molly was aghast. "Why, Mr. Whimple, if she eats that, she won't be able to move at all." Whimple giggled. "Heh-heh-heh. Yes. I know."

Sweetieface never actually appeared on the show, always remaining off-stage as did McGee's favorite telephone operator, Myrt. Although she never got a word in, McGee would find her on the line when he started to make a telephone call and say in apparent surprise: "Oh, is that you, Myrt?"

After that, he would launch into a session of gossip where he told her all the news, or else he repeated the tales she told him to Molly, line by line. "Your brother's up the river again, huh, Myrt?" "Heavenly days!" Molly would exclaim. "Myrt says her brother thinks the fishing is better up the river than any time in years, Molly."

Molly's sottish Uncle Dennis was not quite so removed as Sweetieface and Myrt. He could at least be heard staggering up the back stairs at 79 Wistful Vista.

One of the supporting characters who was less friendly than Myrt or possibly even Sweetieface was the snooty society matron from whom the McGees heard altogether too much. When McGee would make a spectacle out of himself with one of his lamebrain schemes, Mrs. Uppington was sure to appear on the scene. "But Mrs. McGee . . . we simply *cawnt* have your husband making a spectacle of himself . . . He is lowering the tone of the whole neighborhood!" Even tolerant Molly could loose her cool. "Don't give me that Vassar Vaseline, dearie! Next thing you'll get so exclusive you'll want our fire department to have an unlisted phone number!" Mrs. U. would then come back with something devastating like: "Well, *reahhhly*, Mrs. McGee!"

Although Mrs. Uppington did not give them the credit, the McGees actually were somewhat above the economic level of their typical listener. For a time anyway, they had a hired cook and maid in the person of Beulah. She was a black mammy given to a lot of chucklin' and lovin' her white folks. This unrelieved stereotype seemed out of place along Wistful Vista, and the character soon left the show. However, the female impersonator who created Beulah, Merlin Hirt, started his own program about the black woman. After his death, Beulah was played a bit more believably by Hattie McDaniel on radio, and by Ethel Waters on television.

All of these visitors were important and had active fans and partisans. But undoubtedly the most important supporting character ever on the show, and one who like "Beulah" achieved his own show, was the Great Gildersleeve, originally played by Harold Peary.

As with Doc Gamble and Mayor LaTrivia, Gildersleeve and McGee were constantly at each other's throats. The self-satisfied, lovably pompous fat Dutchman would naturally be in conflict with Fibber McGee who always tried to deflate every windbag—except himself. "Now, McGee," Gildy would rumble ominously when Fibber's insults finally began to work through his well-padded hide.

Fibber and Molly were not the no-holds-barred, back alley kind of marital fighters as exemplified in the Bickersons. Molly *tolerated* Fibber's foolishness to a large degree, but occasionally she had to sit on him, just as Mr. Ace had to exercise some control over his foolish wife, Jane. (In Radioland, the quota seemed to be one fool per family.)

The violence between Fibber and Molly was only verbal (only gun-moll type wives on *Gangbusters* ever threw anything at their husbands) and controlled at that. Fibber could only let out his full aggressiveness against Gildersleeve. Partly it was the "you old horsethief" kind of masculine humor that says in effect: We are such good friends, I can say *anything* to you without you becoming permanently offended. But there was a strain of real hostility, too. Both men were posers and pretenders, but McGee always remained as common as an old sweatsock. Gildersleeve had a certain gloss and polish. McGee must have always suspected that perhaps Gildersleeve did have something up his gauntlet where, deep down, he knew that he, McGee, was just a Fibber. They could get into an argument over so simple a thing as McGee crossing the street to mail a letter.

FIBBER: Hiya, Gildersleeve!

GILDERSLEEVE: Hello, McGee! Hey, don't run across that pavement! Can't you see they've just . . .

FIBBER: Aw, go bounce a meatball, you big ape! I know what I'm . . . Hey, what the . . . What is this? Fresh tar!

GILDY: Get out of there, McGee! They've just resurfaced that pavement . . . you'll get stuck!

FIBBER: I *am* stuck! . . .

GILDY: Now now now . . . take it easy, little chum . . . take it easy . . .

FIBBER: Don't "little chum" me, you big chump . . .

GILDY: Why, you ungrateful little grunion! You lippy little lizard! You wait till you get out of there, and I'll teach you a few manners.

FIBBER: Go on . . . you couldn't teach a worm to squirm! You big oaf! By the time I get loose from here I'll be in just the mood to kick you right in the teeth . . . and I don't care if they ain't paid for yet!

MOLLY: Now, now, now, for goodness sakes, boys! Stop it!

Gildersleeve always seemed to have some trick up that sleeve, behind that flashy front, and he came up with one to get McGee unstuck from the tar. As for himself, Throckmorton P. Gildersleeve pulled an even fancier trick out of his cuff: he got himself unstuck from the *Fibber McGee and Molly* show so that he could go on to a show of his own. Gildy left Harlow Wilcox fanatically selling Johnson's Wax and went to his own show where Ken Carpenter sold Parkay margarine. Moreover, he left the domestic strife of the McGees behind him, for the single bliss of bachelor life.

In Gildy's own show, *The Great Gildersleeve,* beginning in 1941, after several years in which he had appeared as a supporting character on the *McGee* series, the pompous Dutchman certainly achieved a higher position in the world

than that of an unemployed tinkerer like Fibber McGee.
Gildersleeve became water commissioner of the neighboring
town of Summerfield, where he set up housekeeping with
his adopted niece and nephew. (Even bachelors seemed to
have to have *some* kind of family life.)

When at last he rose to starring status, the public finally
became aware of the actor who played Gildersleeve: Harold
Peary. The public tends to think that an actor is interchange-
able with the character he plays (the star of TV's *Gunsmoke*
is called Matt Dillon as often as he is James Arness). Peary
had several difficulties in living up to the character he played.
For one thing, he did not even *look* exactly like Throckmorton
P. Gildersleeve, a problem seldom encountered by television
actors. He went on a crash diet to *gain* weight so that he
would more resemble the puffed-up Gildersleeve for publicity photos to promote the radio series, and for several "B"
movies Hollywood produced.

Furthermore, Peary was not Dutch and blustering, but a
scholarly man of Portuguese descent who was adept in five
languages. He was studying medicine, helping out financially
by doing some professional singing, when despite his medical
knowledge the show business bug infected him. By the 1930s,
he was working in Chicago radio, doing roles on comedy
shows, soap operas, and juvenile serials. Among the people
he worked with was Willard Waterman, another young actor.
Producers noted a remarkable similarity in the voices of
Peary and Waterman, and they were often called upon to
double for the other. For instance, both men at one time
or another in the late thirties played the part of Sheriff
Mike Shaw on *Tom Mix*. Both eventually moved to Hollywood and in the early fifties when Peary left *Gildersleeve*
to do a short-lived series he himself owned, *Honest Harold*,
Willard Waterman took over the role of Gildy and played

it for nearly a decade. Waterman did the television series, being plump and mustachioed not unlike Peary, and continued the radio series almost to the end of the fifties, by which time many Americans had forgotten radio still existed.

Writers John Whedon and Sam Moore developed the format of the *Gildersleeve* show when Peary moved away from Wistful Vista. He became a bachelor caring for his orphaned niece and nephew, Marjorie and Leroy (Marylee Robb and Walter Tetley). His Negro maid, Birdie, helped him take care of the home. (Lillian Randolph's Birdie was a much more sympathetic and realistic character than Beulah on the *McGee* show.)

Gildersleeve's world was peopled by strange and amusing characters somewhat similar to those in the world of 79 Wistful Vista. There was Peavey, the peevish druggist (Dick Legrand and later Forrest Lewis), Floyd the opinionated barber (Arthur Q. Bryan), and a number of others. There was, as well, Gildy's parade of girl friends, including one very special girl, the Southern belle, Leila Ransom (played by Shirley Mitchell). Unlike the *McGee* show, these characters did not come up with many clever gag lines; the humor came from character and situation.

Throckmorton P. Gildersleeve was a very good character indeed for humorous situations to spring from. The superficial aspect of his character was his blow-hard act, but beneath it all, you could sense he was sincere and earnest, wanting to help himself and others, but finding that his enthusiasm always exceeded his abilities. In him, we could see ourselves. But unlike us, Gildy could always come up with a laugh over whatever trials he was undergoing—a laugh that rumbled out of his bulging vest and echoed through a million living rooms across the land. The laugh was his trademark, but he had another vocalization that equaled it for fame—his exasperation with his exuberant nephew: "*Leeee-roy!*"

Given these new characters and surroundings, Gildersleeve made a successful move from the *Fibber McGee* show.* *The Great Gildersleeve* proved a most successful spin-off due largely to the fact that it was not simply more-of-the-same as its parent show, *Fibber McGee and Molly*. Both Fibber and Gildy were impractical dreamers, but Gildersleeve had *insides* —he was capable of examining his life and himself, of worry, regret, new and better intentions. He was thoughtful. His show was not as *witty* as McGee's, but it had the appeal of identification which happened in radio usually only on soap operas and adventure serials.

PEAVEY: Hello, Mr. Gildersleeve.

GILDY: Good morning, Peavey! Good morning, good morning, good morning.

PEAVEY: What have you got there, Mr. Gildersleeve?

GILDY: Posters! Just had 'em printed up. I'm going to let you have one for your front window.

PEAVEY: Well, that's real nice . . . Hmm! "The Little Theater in the Dell presents *Cyrano de Bergerac*, starring Throckmorton P. Gildersleeve."

GILDY: That's right, Peavey!

PEAVEY: I didn't know that you had dramatic talent, Mr. Gildersleeve.

GILDY: I didn't know it myself till two days ago . . .

* This was a foreshadowing of the present-day system of "spin-off" shows from television series. Similarly, *The Aldrich Family* and *It Pays to Be Ignorant* began as supporting acts on Kate Smith's variety hour. *Chick Carter, Boy Detective* got his own show, separate from that of his fictional foster father, *Nick Carter, Master Detective*. A late arrival on the radio scene, Batman, was undoubtedly intended to spin off *Superman* but did not land a show of his own until the TV age.

PEAVEY: You know, it's so long since I've been to see a real live play. I used to go all the time, as a younger man.

GILDY: You did?

PEAVEY: Every time Maxine Elliott came to town. I never missed. She was lovely, Mr. Gildersleeve. Lovely . . .

GILDY: That must have been a long time ago, Peavey. Thirty years at least.

PEAVEY: Well, now, I wouldn't say that—I guess it was, though. Thirty years. How times flies! She was lovely!

Of course, Gildersleeve had been talked into doing the role by one of his long line of girl friends, Eve. She had struck at two of his weakest points: susceptibility to a woman's charms and an overweening vanity—a vanity which impelled him to do what in reality he most loathed doing—make a public spectacle of himself. His young nephew could sense that all was not as it should be with this play as Gildersleeve rehearsed.

GILDY: "I doff my chapeau . . ."

LEROY: Would you mind telling me what the story's about?

GILDY: Oh, for heaven's sake! I've told you a thousand times, it's about a man named Cyrano. In this scene, he is fighting a duel. Now be quiet.

LEROY: Okay. Are you gonna do the fighting on the stage?

GILDY: Certainly. Mr. Fairfield showed me all about fencing. One more lesson and I'll be able to cut his head off. Well, let's see . . .

LEROY: Just a second, Unk. What's the duel about?

GILDY: Well, this fellow insulted Cyrano.

LEROY: How?

GILDY: He makes fun of Cyrano's nose.

LEROY: That's very funny!

GILDY: It is not funny. There's nothing funny about it, it's

psychological . . . Cyrano *thinks* he has a big nose. He's very
sensitive about it.

LEROY: I don't get it. Why does Cyrano think he has a big nose?

GILDY: Because it—well, because he has. Leroy, I can't possibly
learn this part if you're talking all the time. Why don't you go
out and play?

As events progressed, Gildersleeve had some second thoughts
about appearing on stage in tights and a big nose, but in
the end, he decided that a member of the distinguished
Gildersleeve family could bring off even so difficult a role.
He wound up insisting he could play the part and even
fought the by then reluctant producer to get on the stage.
The radio show never actually showed it to us but in our
mind's eye, we could see the plump Gildy in tights, equipped
with oversize putty nose, doffing his chapeau.

One could well imagine the comments of Gildersleeve's
rival, the cantankerous Judge Hooker, or how even more
devastating it would be if Fibber McGee had brought Molly
over to Summerfield for the event. In this case, the two old
friends might actually have come to blows.

Time has passed since then. Jim Jordan lives in retirement,
and remarried since the death of Marion. Harold Peary and
Willard Waterman both do feature parts in television. And
Waterman has been on the stage in the long-running Broadway musical comedy *Mame* since its opening in 1966. But
their character creations remain untouched in our memories of the past. Somewhere a rollicking laugh rolls. Somewhere the accumulated junk of a lifetime cascades from a
hall closet. Somewhere there is a place called Wistful Vista
where the greatest conflict we knew was the bickering of two
old friends. But all that is long ago and far away.

3.

Suds in Your Eye

Lorenzo Jones was a lovable bumbling inventor of useless hair restorers and dangerously incendiary bedwarmers. There were a lot of bumblers in radio—Dagwood Bumstead, as his name implied, bumbled through life as *Blondie's* husband, both at home and at his mundane office job; Jane Ace got her speech as tangled up as Lorenzo did some of his inventions. The distinction Lorenzo had was that he did his bumbling in the afternoon, during radio's time period otherwise slotted for weepy soap operas.

Lorenzo was foremost among the less grim breed of sufferers, but he was not alone. Papa David gave out with some Yiddish witticisms on *Life Can Be Beautiful,* as one of many such comedy reliefs in daytime serials. Though there may have been very little intentional humor in *Our Gal Sunday* —with Sunday trying to find happiness as the wife of England's richest and most handsome lord, Lord Henry Brinthrope—

many critics, such as columnist and humorist James Thurber, found Lady Brinthrope's difficulties hilarious. Finally, there were serialized shows that were always regarded as "soap operas" even though they relied almost solely on humor—and often excellent humor at that—including *Vic and Sade*, *Easy Aces*, and *The Goldbergs*.

It was *Lorenzo Jones* among all of these that came closest to combining humor with all the traditional clichés of the soap opera. Since it was written and produced by Frank and Anne Hummert who performed similar tasks for *Young Widder Brown, Backstage Wife*, and others, it naturally bore a family resemblance. Like many others in Soapland, Lorenzo was suspected of murder a half dozen times or so in his life. Of course, people in his home town never really took such accusations against Lorenzo too seriously; they continued to bring their cars into his mechanics shop to be fixed. (If I were involved in a murder every few years, my friends would probably begin to shun me, I feel. But not Lorenzo's loyal neighbors.)

Lorenzo Jones's main activity in life was slightly different from his profession of auto mechanic. He invented things. They weren't big or important—just simple, little items to fill the boredom of life with a series of small disasters. Lorenzo invented a lawn vacuum cleaner, for example, to clean up all the odds and ends from the area surrounding the house—odds and ends such as grass, top soil, garden hoses, anything of value.

On another occasion (proving he knew equally as much about chemistry as he did about mechanics) Mr. Jones devised a sulphur water pep tonic.

Lorenzo's pep tonic did succeed in making people move fast—quickly heading for the equivalent of ship's rails to lean over. And if dissatisfied customers were not enough of a problem, he also had trouble with the local sheriff for peddling medicine without a license. For a law-abiding citizen, Lorenzo had a great deal of trouble simply staying out of jail.

There was a Mrs. Jones, Lorenzo's wife, Belle. His inventions, as the announcer stated each day, had made Lorenzo "a character to the town, but not to his wife, Belle, who loves him." Her contribution to the story often consisted of murmuring "Lorenzo, Lorenzo, I don't know about this . . ." Her favorite time of day was late evening when the lawn vacuum cleaner was put away, and there had been perhaps a final shot of pep tonic. Then she and Lorenzo would lie in their twin beds and quote romantic poetry to each other! These romantic moments seemed to satisfy female listeners that Lorenzo was not a total loss from whom Belle should quickly part.

Jones's employer, Jim Barker, down at the garage, evidently never heard Lorenzo quote poetry and so was incapable of appreciating the finer side of his nature. There came a day when there was one crackpot invention too many and Jim at last regretfully fired Lorenzo.

Lorenzo retreated to his home workshop and perhaps tried to invent a robot to replace garage-owners, while his wife stiffened her upper lip and went out looking for a job for herself. Clever, competent Belle quickly found a position with Madame Cunard's Beauty Salon. When Lorenzo came around to check up on his wife going to work for a madame, the incensed Frenchwoman roundly insulted the luckless inventor. Loyal Belle hotly defended her husband and she, too, got fired—*Zut! Alors!*

It looked like a lean Christmas for the Joneses, but then Lorenzo came home one day with the news he had landed a job as foreman with a firm of building contractors known as Trapp and Sweeney. Naturally, there was something suspicious about anybody who would hire Lorenzo as a foreman. Trapp and Sweeney were a pair of shady characters whose activities got Lorenzo into more trouble with the law. But as always, God seemed to display a special providence for people like Jones, and he got off again. (Presumably by this time, the friendly, local police were punching him in the gut and advising him to "Keep your nose clean.")

Another time, as if Lorenzo's home town was not full enough of con men and desperate characters, a motion picture company moved in to shoot a film on location. Lorenzo's niece-by-marriage, Nellie, was fascinated by show folk, much to the chagrin of her husband, Jones's nephew, Henry.

HENRY: Where were you all morning?

NELLIE: Oh, I was at the "lot"—that's what the motion picture people call the place where they make the picture—it's the "lot" when it's outdoors, and the "set" when it's indoors, Henry.

LORENZO: Say, you ain't being bitten by the theatrical bug, are you, my impressionable niece, are you?

BELLE: Now why don't you two leave Nellie alone. I don't see any harm in her going over there and meeting all those nice people.

HENRY: They aren't nice people, Aunt Belle—they're actors. I've read all about them and their parties.

LORENZO: Are all the actresses there Miss Americas or do you only watch the stronghearted heroes—loosely speaking.

NELLIE: Oh, they are all very hard-working people, Uncle Lorenzo. Mr. Cabot, the director, makes them all work hard. I even met one of the writers of the picture they're making. He has the same worried look you do.

HENRY: Huh—writers, authors. Writers are the worst of all!

NELLIE: They are all very nice to me. Maybe if they learn I

played the lead in the high school play, they will give me a screen test.

LORENZO: Nellie's professional poise was positively uncanny. Why, she was the most unconscious actress I ever saw when she created the difficult role of the wicked stepsister in *Cinderella*.

While Lorenzo and his family disparaged actors and writers, Lorenzo Jones, himself, was the eccentric creative person in a small town, a "character." The small-town radio audience of the forties which worshiped conformity must have got a great deal of satisfaction out of this daily ridicule of the nonconformist.

The writer of the series expertly indulged the audience's prejudices against creative people, while amusing himself with absurdly overstating the situation to the point where the man who wrote the words and the actor who spoke them were condemning themselves. But even so wholesome a program as *Lorenzo* required the use of actors. Belle was played by Lucille Wall (no relation to Lucille Ball, of course) who took matters more seriously when she appeared as the lady lawyer on *Portia Faces Life*. Lorenzo himself was Karl Swenson who seemingly played *half* of the male characters in radio's galaxy of soap operas. Not only Lorenzo, he sounded veddy British as Lord Henry on *Our Gal Sunday*, young and serious as Danny on *Linda's First Love*, and like many people on *Mr. Chameleon*. One suspects that this last show may have been created especially for Swenson by the Hummerts, who also fathered another more famous investigator the kindly old *Mr. Keen, Tracer of Lost Persons*. In it, the detective nicknamed Mr. Chameleon assumed at least one disguise each week and the proper dialect to go with it—Scotch, Irish, hillbilly, whatever.

Frank and Anne Hummert had the ability to create to order any type of radio show that seemed to be required. *Lorenzo Jones* was a custom-made product that tried to follow the successful pattern established by comedy serials that perhaps offered more genuine comment on the American scene.

One of these more substantial entries was *Myrt and Marge*, the story of two girls in show business, family members in the story line, mother (Myrt) and daughter (Marge) in private life. Myrt's real name is Myrtle Vail, a veteran of vaudeville, who marched into the offices of a Chicago chewing gum manufacturer and sold him a show she had written about two young women named Myrt *Spears* and Marge *Minter*. On the first episode, Myrt was leading a line of chorus girls with all the presence of a ranch foreman when a young try-out, Marge, fainted from hunger. She did not recognize the girl, according to the script, because they had been separated for many years (not true in real life for the perennial stage performers). Marge (Donna Damerel, privately Mrs. Peter Fick) died in childbirth at the age of 29, on February 15, 1941, according to the harsh realities of the world, but on the radio series, Marge lived on, afterwards played by Helen Mack. (At this writing, Myrtle Vail lives in retirement.) During the height of its popularity during the thirties, *Myrt and Marge* was touched with more pungent reality than most radio serials. Its theme of "Poor Butterfly" introduced lecherous producers and a sympathetic, effeminate male costume designer. Myrt also gave out with such dialogue as "Listen, you dames, drop that lead and oil up your hips—you know this is the number the Broadway wolves pay twenty-five bucks a seat for, opening night!"

Despite the success of *Amos 'n' Andy* and *The Goldbergs* in the late 1920s, it was *Vic and Sade* beginning in 1932 which achieved the greatest *critical* acclaim among popular comedy serials. Poet Edgar Lee Masters said of the series that it "presented the best American humor of its day." The show was faithfully followed by many other critics and celebrities, reportedly including President Franklin D. Roosevelt. *Vic and Sade* properly had to be experienced. Weeks of listening, or months, or years, were required to fully appreciate all its gentle subtleties. It was *radio* humor, which demanded steady, habitual consumption. Other radio shows and television today generally rely on vaudeville and film techniques concerned with getting laughs over what is happening *now*, without requiring knowledge of what happened weeks or months before. There is nothing comparable to *Vic and Sade* in broadcasting at present, but daily comic strips such as *Peanuts* and *Pogo* offer something of the same appeal.

One episode so resembled another that a side by side comparison of a dozen would seem much the same. Basically, the series concerned Vic Gook and his wife, Sade (a familiar form of "Sadie," no relation to the Marquis de Sade) who lived with their son, Rush, in "the little house halfway up the next block." They were visited from time to time by Uncle Fletcher whose permanent residence was the Bright Kentucky Hotel or various rooming houses.

Vic had an office job. We knew that because he brought paperwork home from time to time. But the part of the lives of Vic and Sade we listened in on concerned the conversations that the couple had around the living room outside of working hours, wherein they discussed such people as Ruthie Stembottom, with whom Sade used to attend washrag sales at Yamelton's Department Store; Jake Gumpos, the garbageman; and the Brick-Mush Man who sold Brick-Mushes to whoever needed them.

During the early years, Vic and Sade held the stage entirely to themselves; not even their son, Rush, appeared on mike. But simple patterns tend to become more complex, and Rush eventually did appear, followed by other speaking characters. Rush was an Establishment kind of kid, seemingly trying to emulate his parents as much as possible. He joined the conversation with recollections of his younger friends, such as Smelly Clark and Blue-Tooth Johnson.

The one somewhat abrasive element in this ideal society was Uncle Fletcher. He seemed to live in a world of his own that could touch any other world only at certain points. There seemed to be a time-lag in his conversation, as if he came from another dimension. He answered questions before they were asked or after three other questions had been presented to him. Since nothing ever seemed to go right for him, he kept reassuring himself that everything was "Fine." "It's the coldest day we've had this year," Sade might observe. "Fine," said Uncle Fletcher. "Would you like one or two spoons of sugar in your lemonade, Uncle Fletcher?" "Fine." Uncle Fletcher also liked to recall his friends and acquaintances, such as the identical twins, Robert and Slobbert Hink and Ishigan Fishigan of Sishigan, Michigan. Regretfully, in discussing some friend of his, Uncle Fletcher would have to add ". . . later died." This was not true of Ishigan Fishigan of Sishigan, Michigan, who used to call him long distance from such exotic spots around the globe as Peoria and Columbus.

In between such phone calls, Fletcher would reminisce.

FLETCHER: Arnie Gupples give Gwendolyn Yowtch this fancy shoe scraper for her birthday. They were engaged to be married at the time. Well, sir, first shot outa the box Gwendolyn went to scrape some mud off her shoes with that shoe scraper, twisted her ankle, had to have the doctor, got mad,

an' give Arnie the mitten. Two months afterwards she married
Art Hungle an' moved to North Dakota. Arnie felt so bad he
quit his job at the shoe store. I heard afterwards he finally
married a rich woman that made him learn to play on the
cornet.

VIC, SADE, RUSH: Umm.

FLETCHER: Stuff happens, don't it?

VIC, SADE, RUSH: Umm . . .

RUSH: Smelly Clark's Uncle Strap likes to talk about the peculiar
junk that takes place in the Universe, an' he says he thinks
that life is controlled by . . .

FLETCHER: Fine! What time's it gettin' to be Sadie? Excuse me,
Vic.

VIC: Not at all.

RUSH: I was the one talkin' . . .

SADE: (*Without conviction*) Oh—early yet, Uncle Fletcher . . .

VIC: Shank of the evening.

Uncle Fletcher did eventually leave. He, Rush, Vic, and
Sade left radio in the mid-1940s, drowned in a sudsy sea
of murder suspects, amnesia victims, and even a few unwed
mothers. Art Van Harvey and Bernardine Flynn played Vic
and Sade, and Clarence Hartzell was Uncle Fletcher in the
scripts by Paul Rhymer.

Vic and Sade unquestionably is the most beloved radio
show of all time with a core of dedicated fans who regularly
write each other letters about their memories of it, test each
other's knowledge with exacting questions, and try to locate
scripts and recordings. *Vic and Sade* told it like it was, but in
reality, it was an anti-Utopia, an idealization of mediocrity.
Those of us who have actually lived in a small town, not
just fantasized about it, know that the mind whose interests
are bounded by a single city block is not that fascinating

or admirable. *Vic and Sade* made wonderful neighbors, but only for fifteen minutes a day.

If *Vic and Sade* were relentlessly small town, the most urbane comedy couple on radio was the *Easy Aces*. The program might well be described as "literate." Goodman Ace wrote the scripts (as well as playing the first-nameless "Mr. Ace" opposite his both real and radio life wife, Jane) and he was and is an American humorist who has been favorably compared to Ring Lardner and E. B. White. His scripts contained such brilliant paraphrases that they have since become new clichés: "time wounds all heels," "in words of one cylinder," and "we're insufferable friends."

These clever remarks were voiced by the supposedly dumb Jane Ace. It is difficult to say whether Jane or Gracie Allen more deserved the title of Mistress of Malaprops and Non-Sequiturs. Both fictional characters projected by the ladies seem to inspire and reflect the other. Goodman Ace was never as dry as George Burns, however. He seemed to suffer more, and acted as if he felt that Jane might shape up some day and act sensible. He was the cynic with the heart of a dreamer. His quiet despair over some foolishness by Jane was usually a forlorn, "Isn't that awful?"

Goodman and Jane Ace began as a team accidentally (as many of the great teams and programs of radio began). In 1930, Goodman Ace was known as "The Movie Man" on KMBC, Kansas City, delivering the intimate gossip of the film world as it could only be known by a resident of Kansas City. One evening, the manager told him that the next act had not shown up, probably drunk again, and Ace had to fill in for another quarter hour. Jane was visiting him and he began talking with her, discussing the bridge game they had had on a previous evening, dissecting some of

Jane's unorthodox plays. The impromptu broadcast drew a lot of favorable mail, and "The Movie Man" did a slow dissolve for a new program with both Aces.

In October 1931 *The Easy Aces* began its network run, originating from Chicago. It was a fifteen-minute program with an unusual time schedule. In most places, it was heard Monday, Friday, and Saturday evenings. (*Mr. Keen* traced lost persons Tuesday through Thursday for the same sponsor.) There could scarcely have been a greater contrast between the witty Aces and the simple-minded Mr. Keen, but the format worked for about thirteen years. After 1944, *Easy Aces* was adapted to a complete half-hour episode once a week, and the title became *Mr. Ace and Jane.*

Other characters appeared in the series from time to time, but the most prominent supporting character was Jane's best friend, Madge (played by Mary Hunter). Madge was the antithesis of Jane, being a calm, levelheaded, resourceful young businesswoman who was never at a loss for words, and always the correct ones. Unlike Mr. Ace, she never really got exasperated with Jane but always took her good-naturedly. Jane, in turn, was much agitated by the fact that Madge was not married. She firmly believed in the best American tradition that every woman should own the labor-saving device of a husband. Around 1935, Madge was engaged to a struggling young artist named Paul. Jane tried everything she could to raise Paul's resources so he and Madge could be married. One day she went to his studio and announced in typical fashion, "I've come to you for an itching, Paul, and every girl in my club wants you to do her, too." Paul etched, but somehow never got up enough scratch to marry Madge.

The Easy Aces always seemed to give the impression they were living on Easy Street, at least compared to most of their listeners. They lived in a pretty nice New York apartment ("Manhattan Serenade" was their theme song) and no doubt swilled cocktails while their listeners drank *Dr. Pepper's*. Jane could even seriously think about buying a mink coat. (Of course, the absurdities she could think about seriously were legion.)

JANE: Now, look, Madge, after he comes in, sits down, and starts reading his evening paper, all I want you to do is start the conversation off by saying: "It certainly is getting cold out; winter isn't far off." You can certainly do that little favor for a pal, can't you?

MADGE: Yes, I suppose so—but what's it leading up to?

JANE: A mink coat.

MADGE: Jane, a mink— . . . Did he say he'd buy you one?

JANE: Not yet. That's where you come in.

MADGE: Me! Now wait a minute, Jane . . .

JANE: Madge, how long have we known each other? . . . Don't say it. I don't like to *think* about all those years, but we started out at school, didn't we? We were playthings. We were always together. Insufferable, weren't we?

MADGE: (*Laughs*) Yes, at times I think we were insufferable . . .

JANE: Damon and Runyon, that's us. And now that I ask you to help me out, you say no . . .

MADGE: But, Jane, why don't you just come right out and ask him?

JANE: Madge, it's easy to see you've never been married . . . I lead up to it in a nice, pleasant roustabout way . . . Before he knows what happened he'll be saying yes.

MADGE: You sure he'll say yes?

JANE: If you do it right. (*Door opens.*) Here he comes. Now don't forget . . . Hello, dear.

ACE: Well, hello, Jane. Haven't seen you in five minutes.

JANE: Yes, it has, hasn't it. Sit down, dear.

ACE: Thank you.

MADGE: Oh. It certainly is getting cold out. Winter isn't far off.
JANE: Speaking of winter, dear, that reminds me—
ACE: No.
JANE: No? No what?
ACE: No new coat.

The comparative affluence of the Aces was as nothing compared to that of the Barbours of *One Man's Family*. They were just damned rich and no two ways about it.

One Man's Family won several awards as the "Best Situation Comedy" on the air for its writer-producer, Carlton E. Morse, but the program was hardly that at all. The *Family* show was also frequently called a "soap opera." Actually it was merely good and unique; there have been few things like it on radio or television. It had elements of comedy, soap opera, adventure, and drama. It was, in effect, a *novel* dramatized for twenty-eight years, beginning in 1932.

Fanny and Henry Barbour lived in Seacliff, California, just outside San Francisco. They had five children: Paul, Clifford, Hazel, Claudia, and Jack, and all of the children eventually had offspring—lots of "bewildering offspring." In Paul's case, there was only an adopted daughter, Teddy. Paul was also unusual in other respects, and was the real center of the story—a World War I ace, later a commercial pilot and sometimes government agent. He was thoroughly embittered with the Establishment, which was actively represented by his own father, Henry Barbour. Much of the humor of the show came from Father Barbour's ultraconservatism.

On one occasion just after World War II, Paul returned home from one of his mysterious trips with a strange woman named Nicollette. Henry Barbour discussed the matter with Paul's adopted daughter, Teddy, who had grown into a young woman herself.

HENRY: Nicollette? Haven't I heard that name before?

TEDDY: You may have, Father Barbour. She's been Paul's traveling companion in South America, the African Gold Coast, and
Central Europe.

HENRY: Traveling companion! ... Nicollette ... Nicollette
Moore. Of course. How does the "Moore" fit in, anyway?
Teddy, that woman's a *foreigner!*

TEDDY: But Father Barbour, such an exciting foreigner! And she's
a friend of the Harlans. Paul met her last spring at the Sky
Ranch when she was staying with the Harlans on King Moun-
tain.

HENRY: Traveling over the face of the earth as Paul's companion!
How'd she finagle that anyway?

TEDDY: She didn't. The government sent her. They didn't even
know they were on the same mission until they met at the
airport. There was no finagling involved.

HENRY: A foreigner! By George, if it isn't one thing, it's another!
What's Paul thinking of, anyway?

Teddy was unusually generous to Paul's "companion,"
Nicollette, since she was herself in love with her foster
father. That may have only been token incest, but later
on, Paul's niece, Joan, expressed much the same taboo love
for him.

All the *Family* members seemed to be a bit atypical.
Father and Mother Barbour were at least unusually rich.
Claudia seemed to show signs of what today we might call
nymphomania, while her twin, Cliff, displayed a comparable
amount of satyriasis. As for the youngest brother, Jack, he
too displayed a fair amount of sexual drive; he fathered six
children (including a set of triplets) hardly by the time he
was of voting age. However, he began to resent so much
responsibility and confessed to Paul a serious if fleeting desire

to murder his children by dropping them off the sea wall into the Pacific Ocean, one by one.

So things went in *One Man's Family*, the "Best Situation Comedy" on radio.

Things were equally less comedic and even more violent in Rushville Center, the setting for *Ma Perkins*. Several people there actually gave in to their murderous instincts. Somehow the guilty ones were never suspected by the towns-people and it was always kindly old Ma or one of her daughters like Fay or Evey who went on trial for the crime, barely escaping the gallows each time.

To relieve the tension caused by the murder trials—or by Banker Pendleton's constant attempts to foreclose on Ma's business establishment, the town lumberyard—Evey (when she was not on trial herself) would make her usual attempts to win the presidency of the Jolly Girls Club. Despite the handicap of having some family member constantly trying to fend off the hangman, Evey occasionally was appointed chairwoman of some committee or other. But the presidency of the Thursday afternoon circle seemed forever denied her. The office was traded back and forth between two of the belledames of the Older Families in Rushville Center. Pleas against the Establishment proved no more effective than usual, and even bribery in the form of mounds of freshly baked cakes and cookies did not sway the electorate. Perhaps Evey even contemplated assassination. Then one of the two permanent presidents moved out of town and the office was finally awarded to Evey. She commented to Ma that life would be downhill after this apex in human existence.

Another recurring moment of humor was the running feud between Ma's son-in-law, Willie, and Shuffle down at the lumberyard. They took turns as to which one of them would come in early and fire up the old coal stove in the office.

(Perhaps The Shadow, if he ever left the city, dropped around from time to time to sell them a load of his sponsor's product, Blue Coal.) Willie was always insisting it was Shuffle's turn and Shuffle was equally as convinced Willie should go. Shuffle usually won because he was a canny old buzzard who could always outargue Willie. Originally, he was just a hired man in the operation, but in later years, Ma referred to Shuffle as her "partner." That says something. One wonders just how close their relationship really was. After all, she had been a widow for a very long time.

Shuffle always had the ability to cheer Ma up in times of trouble, sometimes by pretending to an uncharacteristic denseness. For instance, the time that Fay was widowed at an early age by the death of her husband, Paul:

SHUFFLE: She'll be okay. Remember she's young, Ma . . . In a couple of weeks you'll be taking her down to buy some new dresses, and she'll look at herself in the mirror, and just by accident her eye'll fall on a new hat, and . . . say, you name one woman who can resist the temptation of a new hat, 'specially Fay. She always did have a weakness for the darnedest bonnets I ever saw!

MA: Well, Shuffle, I hope you're right . . . No . . . the thing that's going to cure Fay is . . . is . . . *this.*

SHUFFLE: Eh? What are you waving your hand at . . . what do you mean, "this" . . . you mean old man Johnson raking up leaves there on his front lawn? Evening, Mr. Johnson! Getting deafer 'n' ever, ain't he?

MA: No, I don't mean Mr. Johnson 'specially, but . . . yes, Mr. Johnson among other things. Shuffle, if we'll only look around us, we'll see so much . . . to take the sting out of our sorrows! That's what I meant when I waved at *Rushville Center.* At Mr. Johnson raking his leaves. And the smell of October leaves being burned on twenty lawns . . . Living . . . Taking

the days as they come . . . the seasons . . . living each day
itself . . .

SHUFFLE: I guess that's the story of our lives, Ma . . .

Like all great philosophers, Ma and Shuffle seemed to be
in basic agreement with Father Barbour and Papa David.
There were economic differences between Ma Perkins and
Lorenzo Jones on the one hand, and the Barbours and the
Aces on the other, but they all believed in the same basic,
human values. Sponsors of successful series saw to it that there
would be no "Head-Start" programs to disturb the economic
and philosophical status-quo, and it remained in Radioland
as in the real world, some people were as rich as Henry Barbour and some were as simple as Lorenzo Jones.

4.

So Many Voices

A babble of dialects from the full spectrum of ethnic backgrounds—and a few that had kinship with only some imaginary never-never land—flooded the airwaves in the twenties and thirties. The blackface act of *Amos 'n' Andy* dominated the scene with "Wot am de matter wid yo', Amos?" and it began with the Southern drawl of announcer Bill Hay introducing the two fellows with "Heah they are . . ." Through the crackle and hiss from cathedral-front Philcos, Rudy Vallee sang with his Maine twang, and Russ Columbo's mellow voice was touched with an Italian overtone. British cut-ups like bandleader Ray Noble and comedienne Gracie Fields competed for attention with hillbillies like Judy Canova, Bob Burns, and the Duke of Paduka. Comedians who did not have particularly distinctive voices, themselves, found supporting performers with unusual dialects or inflections. Phil Baker had his veddy British butler, Bottle, and a phantom voice that echoed out of nowhere, Beetle. Ken Murray came up with Oswald, who sounded like a talking walrus.

Your radio antenna became a Tower of Babel whose purpose was not confusion, but clarification. There were so many voices—in a medium that depended on voices alone—that some way to differentiate them was necessary. Further, each dialect, each unique inflection helped us *visualize* the characters in terms of the generalized characteristics of the group to which each dialect spokesman belonged. Everyone knew what a big, dumb Irish cop like Danny O'Neill of *The O'Neills* looked like. Or at least they thought they did.

The thirties were a time of innocence and ignorance and certainly no pair was better suited to it than Lum Edwards and Abner Peabody. With the single exception of *Amos 'n' Andy, Lum and Abner* was the most popular dialect show on radio.

The show dealt with a regional, rather than an ethnic dialect, and represented people who had no pressure group going for them to protest the way in which they were being portrayed—as the country folk from the hills of Arkansas. As "hillbillies," in short.

The series began in 1931 and was centered around the Jot-em-Down Store in Pine Ridge, Arkansas. Both the town and the business establishment were fictional in the beginning, but by 1936, the real town of Waters, Arkansas, changed its name to Pine Ridge and opened up a Jot-em-Down Store of its own.

On the radio show, the Jot-em-Down Store was run by two old-timers, Lum Edwards and Abner Peabody. Both were cranky and querulous, but Abner seemed to be a bit more dense and excitable than his partner. Lum was calmer and more patient and could usually come up with an answer to any problem. Usually it was the *wrong* answer, but it was *an* answer.

Like most successful radio shows, *Lum and Abner* sported a good-sized cast of supporting characters, all of which were played—in the beginning, at least—either by Chester Lauck (Lum) or by Norris Goff (Abner). With a facile larynx, Lauck portrayed Grandpappy Spears, who was even older and more cranky than the two storekeepers; Snake Hogan, who was described as "the salt of the earth," but wasn't; and the even denser handyman, Cedric Wehunt. Goff contributed not only Abner but the grumpy Doc Miller and the old skin-flint, Squire Skimp.

Lauck and Goff had been successful businessmen in Mena, Arkansas, before they became radio performers. Lauck was an auto finance company manager and Goff was secretary of a grocery company owned by his father. In 1931, they took part in a radio broadcast designed to raise funds for flood relief for Mena residents. The two boyhood friends thought of doing a blackface act—they were already good at dialects—but someone else beat them to the punch. In a few minutes' time, they dreamed up the characters of Lum and Abner and ad-libbed their way through a routine. There was so much audience response that the two young men got an immediate audition from the Quaker Oats Company, which put them on the air five nights a week. They remained on radio for over two decades. In later years, they worked for Ford automobiles, Horlick's Malted Milk, General Foods, Alka-Seltzer, General Motors, and many local sponsors, appearing at various times on all four national networks and syndicated to independent stations.

The serial format allowed for the building up of suspense

over several days or even weeks in which some element would develop to its conclusion. One sequence concerned attempts by the ever-scheming Squire Skimp to trick Lum and Abner into selling him some valuable mining stock (or at least stock he *thought* was valuable). Another time, Abner got hold of a copy of *Mechanics Illustrated* and tried to build a robot. Reading matter was dangerous stuff for the two old-timers: On still another occasion, Lum read *Huckleberry Finn* and promptly took Abner with him on a raft down the river.

The original plan had been to send two younger men—Cedric Wehunt and Gomer Bates—out on the journey and then Lum would write up their experiences in a book. But with his usual efficiency, Lum got himself trapped with Abner on the raft as it was swept down the swift stream. They were on the turbulent waters for days with no provisions other than two cases of peanut butter. After a time, privation began to affect Abner's faculties, which were hardly the type to stand much strain.

ABNER: You'd think somebody would have sent out a searching party for us, Lum. Aye doggies, I believe they're just glad to get shut of us . . . Done the whole thing on purpose. Planned every little detail. I bound they're all sitting around laughing, joshing about how they put one over on us . . . Varmits!

LUM: Now don't go imagining a lot of things, Abner . . .

ABNER: 'Lizabeth—my own woman. My own precious life-long partner—turned against me!

LUM: Abner, I believe you're blowing your top.

ABNER: Cedric Wehunt was the one that done it. The boy I trusted with my life. Just like a son.

LUM: Abner, have you been getting into that canned heat? You ain't suppose to eat that stuff.

ABNER: 'Lizabeth, how could you fall for Cedric's awful plan

> . . . Cedric don't love 'Lizabeth. He's just going to marry her to collect my insurance!
>
> LUM: *Marry her?*
>
> ABNER: I can hear 'em talking right now. About me too. Laughing stock of Pine Ridge . . .
>
> LUM: You can't hear no such thing, Abner. You're just worn out from lack of sleep and the cold. Aye grannies, I think you've got a fever.

Eventually, Abner calmed down after he and Lum were rescued. However, for some time after the episode, the mere sight of peanut butter would send him off his nut.

Today, Lum (Chet Lauck) does occasional TV commercials for an oil company in his famous role, while Norris Goff lives in retirement at Palm Springs. The two old friends still see each other regularly and in 1968 they began distributing recordings of their old series to a limited number of radio stations around the country, joining, thereby, a select number of old radio shows such as *The Shadow* and *The Lone Ranger* to have had their recordings survive and to be re-released currently. *Lum and Abner* is the only well-known *comedy* series to be so syndicated. Lauck and Norris's choice of dialect those many years ago was fortunate. What other dialect besides hillbilly could be resurrected today without an avalanche of disapproval?

In discussing the appeal of *The Goldbergs*, Gertrude Berg—who wrote the series and portrayed Molly Goldberg—asked, "Is it because Molly Goldberg, her family and her neighbors are so different from most people, or because they are so much the same? The answer always comes out that it's because we are the same . . . In school . . . my teacher talked of the universality in literature and drama . . . There are surface differences. To me, the really interesting and beautiful thing is that these surface differences only serve to emphasize how much alike most people are underneath."

Gertrude Berg spent many years in demonstrating the appeal to the listener in being able to put his own problems in the context of a different background.

Her program began November 20, 1929, under the title, *The Rise of the Goldbergs*. In that era, categories of programs had not become so neatly pigeonholed and the show fell somewhere between a comedy and what later became known as a soap opera. The dialogue was not composed of outright gag lines but suggested gentle whimsy. The situations similarly fell short of the melodrama of the typical daytime serial. There were no murders, no bouts of amnesia, no "other woman" in the life of the Goldbergs. There was only the one woman, Molly. She dominated the story and her family.

Gertrude Berg had studied writing and acting at Columbia University, but had not really applied herself to those fields after her marriage to the owner of a sugar-processing factory, Louis Berg. When her husband's factory burned in 1929, Mrs. Berg tried to help the family out by getting work in radio. The result was *The Goldbergs*, based on memories of her grandmother. Although the show had ups and downs and was off the air for a year or more at a time, Gertrude Berg was with the series until the early fifties when its success as an early live television series (also by Mrs. Berg) caused its revival on radio once again.

Besides Molly, the Goldberg family included the father, Jake (originally James R. Waters), the children, Rosalie (Roslyn Siber) and Sammy (Alfred Ryder, later Everett Sloane) and Uncle David (Menasha Skulnik). In small roles as neighbors and friends, there were actors who may

have *sounded* Jewish but who certainly did not *look* Jewish
—among them: Joseph Cotten, Van Heflin, and Marjorie
Main. Fans visiting the radio studio were occasionally dis-
mayed to see Paul Kelly standing at the microphone, still
in golf knickers, playing the role of a rabbi.

The program was a liberal education for people in small
towns without large Jewish communities. We learned such
things as that a *yarmulka* was a cap worn at prayer and that
a *cheddar* was a school. The use of real Hebrew and Yiddish
words was plentiful but not as thick in the early days as the
dialect, which reflected the speech patterns of European immigrant Jews.

In one of the earliest episodes, Molly was waiting impa-
tiently for her son, Sammy, to get home.

MOLLY (*Calling up dumb waiter shaft*): Oohoo, oohoo, Mrs.
  Bloom! Is your Mikey home from *cheddar* yet? No? I suppose
  dey must be playing marbles togedder. Yesterday dey had soch
  a fight and today dey're friends again. I tink it would be
  batter far you and far me if dey vould stay mad. Mrs. Bloom,
  you should hear my Rosie playing. She'll be vone in de voild.
  I don't even got to esk her to practice . . . Oy, dere's mine bell
  wot's ringing. It must be Sammy . . .

SAMMY: Hello, mum!

MOLLY: Vat's de matter so late, Sammy? Let me look on your
  hends. Playing marbles, ha? For vat is your fadder slaving for
  vat I'm esking you? A marble shooter you'll gonna be? A
  beautiful business for a Jewish boy!

SAMMY: What's the matter with the marble business? Didn't
  Uncle Morantz pay five thousand dollars just to get his name
  on a piece of marble?

MOLLY: Don't enser me back! If not I'll tell your papa so soon
  he'll come home! Go vash yourself and take de wiolin! No
  vonder is a saying dat in America de parends obey de children.

Twenty years later, in 1949, there had been quite a few changes in the manner of speaking. Now the distinction was more in a unique placement of words, not in a specialized pronunciation. One thing remained the same in the timeless Goldberg home even after twenty years: Rosie was still at her piano.

MOLLY: I'll be right back. And, Rosie, don't forget, I didn't hear you practice. And not less than one hour.

ROSIE: I know, ma. I can't find the dish towel.

JAKE: Where are you going, Molly?

MOLLY: I'll be right back.

ROSIE: Where did you say the dish towels are, ma?

MOLLY: I didn't say yet—nobody gave me the opportunity yet.

JAKE: You also didn't answer my interrogation.

MOLLY: The dish towels are in the kitchen in the lef drawer near the side by the stove.

ROSIE: You used to keep them on the right side.

MOLLY: I changed them—and now Jake, what is your interrogation?

JAKE: Where are you going?

MOLLY: Upstairs.

JAKE: For what?

MOLLY: 5-C wants to see me about something.

JAKE: You were just by 3-C; she wanted to see you about something—3-D, 4-A, 2-G.

One could hope that 5-C would have some suggestion for Molly about what to do with a girl who was still practicing the piano after two decades and had not yet landed a husband.

After the success of a book called *How to Be a Jewish Mother,* Gertrude Berg was called upon to record an album with the same title. She, of course, was the *ultimate* Jewish mother. Satirist Jules Feiffer has commented that he could accept the comic-strip world of *Wonder Woman* where women were super-powerful and all men ineffectual after growing up at the hands of his own Jewish mother. Molly Goldberg was a kind of domesticated Wonder Woman who seldom left the kitchen; a sort of female Lone Ranger. She dispensed wisdom, advice, and stirring patriotic word-poems. "Anybody which reveals military information is a *killer* with the blood of our young men on her hands," Molly cheerfully told a twelve-year-old neighbor girl who revealed her dad was having to work late at the plant during World War II.

Even after *The Goldbergs* faded from the air, Gertrude Berg continued to write books, appear on the Broadway stage, and do another television series, *Mrs. G. Goes to College*. The "G" did *not* stand for Goldberg, but it might as well have. Gertrude Berg died in 1966. It is doubtful that anyone else would have the temerity to play Molly Goldberg ever again.

In 1931, and until the rise of the Nazis contributed to the decline of comic German-types, Jack Pearl's Baron Munchausen was one of the very top radio comedians. Everyone listened to the Baron spinning an outrageous tale of adventure to his straight man, Sharlie (Cliff Hall). If Sharlie expressed any doubt as to the story's authenticity, the Baron was sure to put him down with "Vas you dere, Sharlie?" The phrase was used as often and as incongruously as "Sock it to me" is today.

From an obscure vaudeville comic, Jack Pearl rose to be one of the highest paid stars in all of show business. He not only appeared on his own show, but on the biggest variety show in radio, *The Fleischmann's Yeast Hour* starring Rudy Vallee. Vallee was a cool, self-contained figure in a hot, frantic era. He could sing "I'm Just a Vagabond Lover" with nasal passion; he could deliver lines (even commercials) believably; and he occasionally managed to get a few laughs himself.

VALLEE: You tell some remarkable stories, Baron. That last one was so fishy it gave me a haddock.

BARON: Der Baron makes mid der jokes . . . Dat's very *finny*, Mr. Vallee . . . Now der last time I vas in Souse America—

VALLEE: I know—you dived down to the bottom of the harbor at Rio, and there were Lou Holtz and I playing Cassino . . .

BARON: Honestly, I don't know how you can lie like dat!

VALLEE: Forgive me, Baron. So you were in South America. How was the swimming down there?

BARON: Pretty rough—until I reached Miami.

VALLEE: You swam to Miami? Unbelievable!

BARON: I make very gudt time too—a shark was pushing me.

VALLEE: I still don't believe it.

BARON: Then the shark swallowed me.

VALLEE: Incredible!

BARON: Where do you think I phoned you from? . . . I swam and swam and swam and vun day I saw a wave over a thousand feet high.

VALLEE: A thousand feet high!

BARON: Sure. It vent up in the air over a thousand feet and stayed dere—it vas a permanent wave!

The Baron did not know the perfect put-down for Vallee, which was a line used years later on another show by an elevator operator being harassed by Vallee. "Look," he said, "you don't tell me how to do my job, and I don't tell you how to love vagabonds!"

Jack Pearl continued doing his Baron Munchausen act intermittently for years, doing much the same routine on the

Jackie Gleason television show in the middle sixties. But aside from the unpopularity of comic Germans, a world that was capable of either blowing itself up or traveling to the stars was no longer impressed by tall stories that were dwarfed by the daily newspaper. We were no longer amused by the fantastic. We were merely taxed for it.

Some comedians invented purely fictional "dialects" for themselves. The most famous and beloved of these comedians from the early years of radio with his own distinctive speech pattern was Joe Penner. His career was relatively brief, but during it he was at the top. His catch lines became household words: "You nar-rr-schty (nasty) man!" and "Wanna buy a duck?" and "Don't you ever *do* that!"

Unfortunately, Joe Penner's humor was almost entirely in *how* he said it, not in what he said. He sounded like one of Red Skelton's characters or an uptown Mortimer Snerd—except that Penner was being himself. All comedians, it has been said, ask us for sympathy. A few like Penner, and the silent screen's Harry Langdon, seemed to ask us for outright pity.

His humor hardly stands well without his unique delivery.

PENNER: What's the best way to raise corned beef and cabbage?
MAN: I dunno, Joe.
PENNER: With a knife and fork!
MAN: Now, listen, Joe—
PENNER: What kind of hen lays the longest?
  A dead one! Yuk, yuk, yuk!

Ed Wynn resembled Joe Penner in sounding very peculiar, but his humor was not entirely in his lisping, shrill delivery. He created and selected material carefully, and his own magnetic charm carried him over a career much longer than that of Penner and many other comics from the pioneering days of radio.

As a one-shot special, Wynn broadcast his stage play *The Perfect Fool* as early as June 12, 1922, which (so far as is known) was the very *first* radio comedy show with a full cast. However, his stage career kept him busy until 1932 when he began his first regular series as the *Texaco Fire Chief*. Wynn had always spoken on the stage in a natural, middle range voice. "But the night of the first 'Fire Chief' broadcast I was pretty well keyed up," Wynn once reported. "When I rushed out and started to speak, it was in that high register, and unconsciously I stayed with it through the broadcast . . ." And throughout the years that followed.

As the Fire Chief, he worked with Graham McNamee, the popular announcer who also doubled elsewhere as a sportscaster and special events reporter.

WYNN: As the curtain goes up on the opera, *Carmen,* you see Carmen, the heroine of the opera. She is very pretty but very thin. She is so thin she's just like a bone; in fact her own dog buried her three times in one week. . . . The gypsies gather around the fire just as the hero enters. His name is Joesay.

GRAHAM: You mean Hosay. It isn't pronounced "J" in Spanish; it's pronounced "H".

WYNN: Oh, that's ridiculous, Graham. According to that if you saw a donkey pulling a carriage in Spain you'd call it a "hack-ass." Well, all right, Graham, I'll say Hosay but it sounds silly to me . . . She says, "So you are a bullfighter. Have you any scars?" and Hosay replies, "I don't have any scars on me but I can let you have a cigarette." *Soo-ooo-ooo.* . . . Carmen kisses him but she forgets to take the cigarette out of her mouth . . . This kindles a spark in the bullfighter and he realizes he loves Carmen and he proposes to her . . . *Soo-ooo-ooo* . . .

The last act of the opera takes place in Madrid, Spain. It is the day before the bull fight . . . He says, "Carmen, how can you treat me like this? After all, I have given you the ten best years of my life." And Carmen says, "My goodness, were they your best?"

Nearly a decade and a half later, radio had changed a lot, but Ed Wynn hadn't, even though he no longer called himself "The Fire Chief." He was now known as King Bubbles, monarch of *Happy Island.*

ANNOUNCER: What are you laughing at, your majesty?

WYNN: The darndest thing happened. I was just carrying a jar of jelly wrapped in a newspaper when it fell on the floor and broke. You should see the jam Dick Tracy is in today!

ANNOUNCER: So you have Dick Tracy on Happy Island, eh? In America we even have him on the radio.

WYNN: Don't talk to me about American radio. The programs never have the right sponsors. If I had my way, bald-headed men would sponsor *Can You Top This,* waiters in restaurants would sponsor *Take It or Leave It,* and the right program for women who can't get girdles, *Let Yourself Go* . . . Tonight's story is called *The Common Cold.* Isn't that a catchy title? . . . Our heroine reminds you of radio programs . . . Her face shows *The March of Time,* her figure is like *We the People,* and her nose is like a pelican's—it's *Just Plain Bill.*

Ed Wynn was not content to remain on *Happy Island* forever. He went on to a career as a dramatic actor on television and in movies, continuing to earn the applause he so appreciated. His one defect as a radio comedian may have been his use of stage techniques—such as changes of costumes and funny hats—to get laughs from the *studio* audience watching him, but to which the audience listening at home could not relate. Wynn, incidentally, was the *first* to use a live studio audience for his broadcasts, a major innovation in radio, one of the innovations of Ed Wynn that continue to influence broadcasting.

The influence of the funny voice or the dialect has grown less and less important in radio and television. In a short-lived series long after the Golden Age of radio comedy, in the late fifties, Stan Freberg used Mexican bandits or German Nazi officers in his sketches who always made a point of saying "I'm Swiss. That way, we don't offend anybody." Except maybe the Swiss.

Today, there may be a tinge of guilt at the thought that we could have laughed at immigrants or people with embarrassing speech patterns. We live in an up-tight world where we are afraid to laugh at anybody and where everybody resents being laughed at. Yet each of the minority groups tells much the same kind of jokes on itself as were offered by old time radio. Perhaps someday we will once again let each other in on the jokes about ourselves, as we did in those Depression days when we were all in the same leaky boat.

5.

Kingfish and Co.

Amos 'n' Andy was *the* dialect show of the good old days of radio, a program fondly remembered by "everybody." A more generous estimate might even place *Amos 'n' Andy* as a part of our national folklore. In any case, it existed on radio for over thirty years! The value of its existence to society and to the arts must be left largely to the judgment of both history and each individual. While its speech patterns were doubtlessly inaccurate exaggerations at .best, and were offensive to many Negroes, it should be noted that the program veered *away* from the harsher stereotypes of the time. If *Amos 'n' Andy* had been any *more* favorable to the Negro, it simply would not have been allowed to get on the air, let alone stay on the air, in the climate of public misinformation that prevailed in the 1920s and 1930s. The Negro community in general responded favorably to the program, starved as it was for any recognition at all by the mass media.

Much of the public, black and white, assumed that *Amos 'n' Andy* were, or were played by, genuine Negro performers. Eventually, it became public knowledge that the whole show was performed by two young white men, Freeman Gosden doubling as Amos and the Kingfish, and Charles Correll as Andy and various other roles.

Amos 'n' Andy was, in more than one way, a study in black and white. Amos was the most priceless of men, and Andy was the most worthless. Andrew Brown's vanity, ignorance, and laziness contrasted sharply with Amos Jones's practical intelligence, passion for hard work, and love and respect for family.

The conflict between Amos and Andy was classic. It was the guy who knows all the angles (and how to cut the corners) out to take the square. Oliver Hardy got Stan Laurel to push the piano up the hill for him by pulling on the front side with one finger. Mr. Dithers got Dagwood to work all night on the new blueprints because there might be a raise in it for him. Jack Benny got Kenny Baker or Dennis Day to mow his lawn for him by telling him that Benny had lost a lucky silver dollar in the high grass. And Andy Brown got Amos Jones to clean up their room by saying he had lost a letter from his Uncle Henry which told where they could get a job.

AMOS: I don't see dat letter 'round here.

ANDY: Keep lookin', son.

AMOS: I don't see it.

ANDY: Well, you ain't lookin' in the right spot. Try sweepin' out from under the bed.

AMOS: Well, ain't you even going to get out of the bed while I does the sweepin'?

ANDY: I'se restin' my brain, Amos. The muscles in my head needs recapitulation.

We all got a chuckle out of a situation like that because we had all been in the same spot. Who had not found himself foxed into a bad corner by the fellow next to you at work, your brother-in-law, the boss, your wife, your husband, a salesman, a customer?

Amos's one fault may have been that he was too naïve to be fully believed, while the major drawback to Andy was that he really wasn't crooked enough for sufficient contrast. Clearly something was needed and so the character of George Stevens was introduced. Stevens was "Kingfish" of the Mystic Knights of the Sea lodge. Most people simply called him "Kingfish."

The Kingfish was definitely a shady character, no two ways about it. He was an out-and-out crook, but not really clever enough and occasionally too soft-hearted to make a success out of being a confidence man.

On the twenty-fifth anniversary program, there was a dramatized re-creation of Andy's first encounter with Kingfish—the way Andy remembered it.

ANDY: Say, s'cuse me for protrudin', stranger, but ain't you got a hold of my watch chain?

KINGFISH: Your watch chain? Well, so I does. How you like dat? One of dese solid gold cufflinks of mine musta hooked on your watch chain dere.

The story was probably apocryphal, Andy's joke at the Kingfish's expense. Kingfish never stooped to outright theft. It required too much physical activity, and it was too straightforward to appeal to his devious wits.

It would seem that simple, trusting Amos would be the natural victim for the scheming Kingfish, but he was not. Amos proved W. C. Fields' contention that "you can't cheat an honest man." Amos had no interest in get-rich-quick schemes. He was confident that he could get ahead in this world through good, hard, honest work. Only Andy could be tricked into buying the gold watch that Kingfish had to unload at "a sacrifice, son, a powerful sacrifice."

And we laughed. Laughed at a crook? Laughed at such greed and stupidity? Ah, but we said to ourselves: "It isn't *we* who are that dumb, *we* who are that crooked. But aren't *they* funny?"

Before Kingfish came to dominate the series, it was Andy who was the most devious character around, figuring out a million ways to inveigle Amos. Andy would show him how they could indisputably gain control of the entire chewing tobacco market of Chicago by growing the stuff in the window boxes of their rooms. "Ain't dat somethin'?" Amos would marvel. Then when the plants turned out to be poison ivy, all he could do was cry, "*Awaa-awaa-awaaa!*" It was a cry of anguish and despair echoed by many other people during the thirties, both off and on radio. Mike Clancy gasped, "Saints preserve us, Mr. Keen!" Molly Goldberg murmured, "Oy Vey!" Jack Benny dead-panned, "*Well!*" But for Amos, it was "*Awaa-awaa-awaa!*"

Andy Brown was always at the ready with a scheme for sudden wealth, which always somehow involved Amos doing a lot of hard work which Andy could oversee, in the manner of a business executive or a book publisher. It was necessary for Andy to conserve his intellectual capacity a great deal of the time in a horizontal position. But even when Andy ordered Amos about, belittling him, and taking credit for all of Amos's hard work and solid ideas, Amos never seemed to think he was being treated in any way but fairly by his best friend.

Andy was not always as generous toward Amos. If Amos

somehow failed to move the piano up the hill all by himself and had a melodically tinkling disaster, Andy would rumble in a slow baritone: "I'se regusted with you, Amos!"

Leaving church one Sunday, Amos met Ruby Taylor and they clicked right from the start. She was sweet, pretty, and completely devoid of "dialect" as the daughter of a moderately wealthy Chicago businessman who owned a large garage. Obviously, she was highly desirable, and Amos was to have several rivals.

The first to try to come between Amos and Ruby was a fellow so lovesick that he robbed the safe at the garage and tried to make it look as if Amos were the guilty man. Andy and Amos's other loyal friends worked day and night during a serial sequence and finally found the evidence that cleared Amos and convicted his rival.

This was only the first such scheme to put Amos in jail, and to try to capture Ruby's heart during his absence. The next to try it was "The Kid," quite apparently a white man, who hungered after the Negro girl. Such an idea was certainly a bit "daring" for the time, as it would be even today in commercial broadcasting.

To win Ruby, "The Kid" worked with his partner, Spud, to throw the guilt for the theft of some valuable furs onto Amos. The two crooks discussed the matter in Spud's hotel room.

SPUD: You get Amos messed up in this thing, so you can get him framed into the pen, you see, and you get his gal, that's all you want to do . . .

"KID": Now there you go talking about me wanting a dame. Say, how about the time you bumped off that guy in Philadelphia?

SPUD: Ah, let it alone.

"KID": I guess that was on account of a dame too, wasn't it?

> . . . Now listen, Spud, what's the use of you sitting up here
> turning gray-haired on account of something that's all set. This
> kid Amos is going to jail . . . (*FADE*)
>
> AMOS: Andy, I don't know what I going to do. The lawyer's get-
> ting uncouraged about it.
>
> ANDY: Amos . . . That ain't "uncouraged"—it's "de-couraged" . . .
>
> AMOS: But . . . you know, Andy . . . we kind of go along living
> . . . we don't 'preciate what we got. We don't 'preciate we
> can walk down the street, there ain't nobody there with a gun
> to shoot you, or try to put you in jail . . . If I go to the
> pennitencery, how sad it going to be . . . to think of all the
> pretty things outdoors in the summertime . . . trees . . .
> green grass . . . You know, Andy, takes something like this to
> make you stop and think that you is well off that everything is
> just goin' along . . .

It was a young attorney who uncovered the evidence to
clear Amos and convict the criminals. Andy tried to help,
even going so far as to study a law book. Unfortunately, it
turned out he had been mistakenly studying a book on the
"Law" of Gravitation.

This fur robbery sequence, from July 1929, reveals many of
the major aspects *Amos 'n' Andy* would present for years to
come. There was romantic trouble over a girl; a confidence
game or racket; Andy's bungling denseness, and finally,
Amos's simple philosophy. (In the vacuum of early radio,
even simple philosophies became profound.)

The strong element involving actual gangsters finally van-
ished after a number of years. But in the twenties and
thirties, the appearance of underworld characters marked
not so much an intrusion of escapist fiction as an expression
of everyday reality. During Prohibition, the most mundane
citizens were required to deal with criminals to get potables
for a party, or to accept other goods or services from them.

Kingfish and Co.

Amos and Andy did not, as far as is known, ever have to pay protection money on the business they started, the Fresh-Air Taxicab Company of America, "Incorpulated." It was the company's single cab that Amos was driving the night he was framed for the fur theft. The car had a remarkable facility for falling apart, and not at the most convenient times, such as before Amos drove to the incriminating location. The cab's fenders fell off, the doors fell off, the headlights fell off, and one might assume business fell off. The vehicle's very worst fault may have been the tendency to *explode*. Gasping for breath as he emerged from still another automotive disaster, Amos would again cry, "*Awaa-awaa-awaaa!*"

The office of the Fresh-Air Taxicab Company ("Fresh-Air" since naturally the cab did not have a roof) seemed luxurious by comparison. It contained one desk, one swivel chair where the president of the corporation could "rest his brains," one telephone on which to answer occasional calls for cab service, and one soap box to entertain frequent guests—like Lightnin', who did not really seem to live up to his name when it came to speeding toward work; or the Kingfish, who could watch Amos and Andy at their honest jobs all day.

The only thing Andy liked better in that office than the swivel chair was the swivel-hipped secretary he had hired, one of his countless girl friends. She was Miss Blue. They spent a great deal of time talking to one another, on the office intercom system. The trouble was that Lightnin' had installed the system defectively so that it would work only one way, from the secretary's office *to* Andy's office. So to initiate a conversation, Andy had to yell out loudly, "Buzz me, Miss Blue!" Soon the whole country was echoing that call.

Aside from Miss Blue, Andy fared far worse in his romantic entanglements than did Amos with his single romance with Ruby. A breach-of-promise suit brought against him—based on some letters he had written—by "Madam Queen" in the early thirties gained the show its highest audience rating. During this time, theater owners actually stopped movies and piped in the *Amos 'n' Andy* radio broadcast live. In fact, it was possible to walk down a small town street in the summer and not miss a line of *Amos 'n' Andy* as the show spilled out of open windows from every house on the block.

The prototype of the famous breach-of-promise case came a few years earlier when the show was just beginning. In this original sequence, Andy was being sued by a character called the Widow Parker. She was rather successful at catching husbands. She had had five before, but Andy was reluctant to make it an even half dozen.

Just before the 1928 case went to trial, faithful Amos was with Andy and his attorney, Spielman. The lawyer was trying to coach Andy how to behave on the witness stand.

SPIELMAN: Now, Brown, you can occasionally use the expression "I don't remember." Don't make it noticeable, but occasionally say, "I don't remember." Now, don't forget that. Now, what are you going to say?

ANDY: "Now, don't forget dat."

SPIELMAN: No, no: "You don't remember."

ANDY: Oh, dat's right; "You don't remember."

SPIELMAN: No, no: "*I* don't remember."

ANDY: You don't remember what?

AMOS: No, no, Andy. Listen, "*You* don't remember."

ANDY: Oh, oh! Who is my lawyer?

SPIELMAN: Now, Brown, just say, "I don't remember."

ANDY: Ain't it some way dat I can keep off o' dat chair again up

1. Charlie McCarthy is being spoofed by comic Ken Murray as Charlie's guardian, Edgar Bergen, looks on. Both men seem to have borrowed Charlie's mode of dress for this World War II era publicity shot.

2. W. C. Fields and Mae West talking into a modern telephone on the set of their 1940 comedy-Western, *My Little Chickadee*. This movie partnership was encouraged by an appearance on a Bergen-McCarthy broadcast in which the couple created sensational head-lines.

3. Red Skelton as "Deadeye," one of his famous radio creations, still going strong in this 1965 television sketch with singer Johnny Mathis.

4. Red Skelton and his whole 1949 radio cast: standing (from left to right) are announcer Pat McGeehan, the Four Knights singing group, bandleader Dave Rose; seated are Verna Felton ("Grandma"), actor Rod O'Connor, Lurene Tuttle ("Mother"), and front and center, Red himself.

5. Eve Arden as "Our Miss Brooks" casts a quizzical eye at the poster of Gale Gordon as Osgood Conklin in the 1956 feature film version of the radio and television series.

6. Fanny Brice as Baby Snooks mugs with total lack of inhibition for the NBC series, *Good News of 1939*. This variety series eventually was entirely taken over by the Snooks sketch.

7. Gertrude Berg as Molly and Philip Loeb as Jake re-create their radio and television roles in the 1950 movie, *The Goldbergs*.

8. Bud Abbott and Lou Costello are listening intently to something —a radio perhaps—behind that office door in a scene from their 1947 Universal film, *Buck Privates Come Home*.

9. Fibber McGee and Molly pose for the NBC cameraman in 1945. Their real names were Jim and Marion Jordan but they were never identified as other than Fibber and Molly even in cast credits.

10. Harold Peary, the original Great Gildersleeve, watches the results of his magnificent billiard shot as Fibber McGee looks on in consternation in this still from the 1942 movie, *Here We Go Again,* one of several Hollywood films they made together.

11. Karl Swenson, famous as the comic inventor, Lorenzo Jones, also appeared with this unidentified actress on a more serious soap opera, *Our Gal Sunday,* in 1937.

12. Ed Wynn, a Broadway comic who went on to great success in radio as the *Texaco Fire Chief* and King Bubbles on *Happy Island*.

dere? All dese peoples in the court room looks at me when I get up dere. I feels rebarrassed.

SPIELMAN: No, no, you *must* get up there, but remember, "I don't remember."

ANDY: "Remember I don't remember." I got-cha.

Naturally, Andy forgot not to remember.

Fortunately for Andy, the evidence was finally ruled inconclusive.

When Andy ran into a similar situation with Madam Queen a few years later, events built to a stronger climax. It seems difficult to believe in these days when we follow hourly news bulletins to see if some particular crisis is going to mean the end of human life on this planet, but in the early thirties, an entire nation could be held spellbound for weeks to find out if a fictional character was going to lose a breach-of-promise suit. Events seesawed back and forth for days. A witness would exonerate Andy. His evidence would be destroyed in cross-examination. A good point would be made for Andy. He would ruin it all, himself. Finally, the big moment came. Madam Queen herself would testify. She mounted to the stand. This would cinch it one way or another. Her attorney stepped forward to ask the first question. Suddenly, Madam Queen screamed and slumped to the floor.

That was on a Friday. Over the weekend thousands upon thousands of letters, telegrams, phone calls flooded the stations carrying the show demanding to know what had happened. No one could possibly wait until Monday to find out. Police stations were called for inside information. Press services tried to find out from Gosden and Correll ahead of time. But after all that, the country still had to wait until Monday when it was revealed that—

Madam Queen had seen the husband she had thought

dead sitting in the back of the courtroom. She was in no position to sue anybody for breach of promise.

Case dismissed!

It was no wonder that Andy did not want to get married. He had the horrible example before him of his friend, the Kingfish, and Kingfish's wife, Sapphire. Sapphire spent her life in one long shrewish insistence that Kingfish get an honest job. However, the Kingfish found all his time occupied with his lodge duties at the Mystic Knights of the Sea. He enjoyed organizing committees, interpreting by-laws, and—best of all—collecting dues. (In the early days, the Kingfish had the assistance of such brother officers as the Swordfish, the Shad, the Whale, and the Mackerel, but the only trace left of these by the forties was in the Kingfish's oft-repeated exclamation, "Holy Mackerel, Andy!")

As Kingfish grew more important to the show, the old drawn-out serials seemed less effective, perhaps because unless it was shown in a single episode that the Kingfish's attempts to hustle his friends like Andy actually came to nothing, or even to their benefit, he might seem too unsympathetic. In any case, in February 1943, *Amos 'n' Andy* went off the air after fifteen years of regular broadcasts. The two stars took stock of where they had been, and where they were going. They would be back.

The team that was to become Amos 'n' Andy first got together in the real world on August 12, 1919, at a lodge hall. Kingfish was nowhere around. This was the Elks, not the Mystic Knights of the Sea.

Charles Correll was staging a musical for the F.O.E. in Durham, North Carolina. He tried some of the local talent and realized quickly that he needed outside professional

help. He placed a long-distance call to the home office of
the talent agency for whom he worked. His call was answered by another new employee, Freeman Gosden, who
took the job for himself. While Gosden's regular work was
as a magician's assistant, he was handy with the ukulele and
the boys in Durham opined they had never heard better.
After the show, Correll approached Gosden with compliments
on his work. The two liked each other immediately and
from that day on, they virtually worked not a day that was
not in partnership for over forty years. In 1969, they are still
friends, still planning new broadcasting ventures together.

Correll is the older of the two, having been born in 1890
in Peoria, Illinois, nearly a decade before Gosden's voice
first hit the air with a wail in Richmond, Virginia, in 1899.
Both had Southern backgrounds. (Correll's family had moved
up from the Deep South during reconstruction.) The South
influenced even their natural speech patterns, as well as the
exaggerated dialect of their characters. The "Southern" attitude, however, did not affect their own personal philosophy. Though they never either tried to herald or conceal the
fact they were white they identified themselves so completely with the Negro race that most people thought they
actually were Negroes.

Radio was still the "wireless" or the Marconi instrument
when the two first met. The medium was still very experimental in 1920 when Gosden and Correll's theatrical tour took
them to New Orleans. A then unnamed radio station was
making trial broadcasts and its manager invited the two men
to come on over after their stage show and sing a song. They
tried out the popular number, "Whispering," on the very first
broadcast they ever made together. Results were good. One
listener all of four blocks away reported the broadcast came in

loud and clear, picked up by the cat's whisker of her crystal set.

Their next radio job was not for free. They got a solid meal from the manager of WEBH in the Edgewater Beach Hotel in Chicago for doing a program of songs around 11:30 each evening. At times, that meal was the only one they got all day.

In November 1925 the manager of the Chicago *Tribune* station invited the two men to stop by and see him about appearing on a really powerful station. They would absolutely have to be paid in cash, they decided. *Fifteen dollars a week,* Gosden suggested. Not a cent less. Correll was unimpressed. They would, he pointed out, be lucky to get ten dollars each. Gosden came down to earth and agreed.

The two men walked into the office of manager Harry Sellinger, grimly muttering to themselves "ten dollars, ten dollars."

"Fellows," Sellinger reportedly said, "how would you like to work for WGN at $125 a week?"

"Ten—ten—tentatively, *yes,"* one of the pair allegedly managed to say.

For their salary, they had to work from 10 A.M. to 2 A.M. the next morning—announcing, singing songs, playing the piano, telling jokes, writing and delivering sketches. The two worked themselves thinner than when they had been eating only one meal a day.

WGN executive Ben McCanna next showed up with a beaming smile and a new offer. How would the boys like to dramatize one of the *Tribune* comic strips? Say, *The Gumps?*

The two men thought over the problems of broadcasting their version of Sidney Smith's famous cartoon strip. It dealt with married life—and neither was yet married—and it would call for the "uppity" accents of the stereotyped rich man. All in all, they figured they could do a better job with the minstrel show dialects they had used in their theatrical tours.

Gosden and Correll developed two Negro comedy characters all their own called *Sam 'n' Henry*. The program went on the air in January 1926 with Freeman Gosden playing the loud-mouth braggart opposite Charles Correll as the more easygoing character.

The show was so successful they got a better offer from the Chicago *Daily News* station, WMAQ. However, WGN owned all rights to the names, *Sam 'n' Henry,* and would not release them. Gosden and Correll had to come up with new names for their characters. One legend has it that as they left the office after being signed for the new series, Gosden and Correll entered an elevator operated by a man named Amos. When they got to the lobby, they saw the janitor, Andy, at work. Whether or not this was really their source, the chosen names worked well, familiar from minstrel shows about similar stock figures.

The first broadcast of *Amos 'n' Andy* came on March 19, 1928. Gosden and Correll did everything. They played not only Amos and Andy but every other character, male or female. They wrote their own scripts, supplied their own sound effects, timed their own shows, and probably even emptied their own wastebaskets.

Other stations wanted to carry the show, as well as WMAQ. The series became the first syndicated program in radio, even before the advent of the standard method of syndication: the sixteen-inch, 33⅓ rpm transcription disc. In 1928, *Amos 'n' Andy* put the main body of their fifteen-minute shows on two twelve-inch phonograph records. The local station announcer still had to read the opening, the commercials, and sign-off.

Gosden and Correll's idea for a "chainless chain" (as they called the series of stations playing their shows) was inventive, but *Amos 'n' Andy* was too good for the idea of syndicating recorded programs, generally only used in later years for cheaply produced mystery shows.

The *Amos 'n' Andy* show proved of coast-to-coast network quality. The fledgling National Broadcasting Company hired Gosden and Correll for $100,000 a year. Their first network broadcast (for Pepsodent toothpaste) came August 19, 1929.

The series was on six nights a week for a time, then five, first at 11 P.M., and finally at an earlier hour, 7 P.M. (Eastern Time) so that the whole family could hear it. And whole families listened, many families. The show had forty-two million listeners when there were just over one hundred million people in the nation.

The fifteen-minute series for Pepsodent lasted until 1937, when Gosden and Correll picked up a new sponsor, Campbell Soups, and moved the studio location for the series to Hollywood. (In the storyline, Amos 'n' Andy moved east instead of west—to New York's Harlem.) As the locale of the series changed, so did the theme song, from "The Perfect Song" to "Angel's Serenade."

When Campbell Soups sponsorship ran out in 1943, the two comedians vacationed a few months and revived the show as a complete half-hour story once a week for Rinso Soap Flakes, and later Rexall Drug Stores. In addition, Gosden and Correll no longer did the majority of their own writing. Bob Connolly and Bill Moser became the chief writers and later executive producers.

Toward the end of their long run, Amos and Andy joined with the Kingfish to become disc jockeys on *The Amos 'n' Andy Music Hall*, playing popular records, interspersed with bits of some kind of storyline as they discussed the events of their day. This final Amos 'n' Andy series came to an end just after Thanksgiving 1960, because of a policy change at CBS against dramatized radio programs.

It was this policy change at CBS that canceled the *Amos 'n' Andy* radio show, not agitation from civil rights groups, as has been erroneously reported. If nothing else, the radio show helped give jobs to Negroes in radio. When broadcasters found the public would accept *supposedly* Negro entertainers, real Negroes found work, such as Rochester on *The Jack Benny Show* and Eddie Green in *Duffy's Tavern*, each of whom were portrayed as both intelligent and virtually free of dialect. In later years, Gosden and Correll stopped playing all the roles themselves and other actors, many of them black, were added to the cast—notably the fine comedienne, Ernestine Wade, as Kingfish's wife, Sapphire.

Miss Wade was the only carryover of the radio cast to television. Gosden and Correll produced the TV version of *Amos 'n' Andy* which featured the black actors, Alvin Childress as Amos, Spencer Williams as Andy and Tim Moore as Kingfish.

Now that the public could actually see Kingfish & Co., there were complaints from the National Association for the Advancement of Colored People and other groups. Kingfish was shady. Andy was shiftless. And legal groups were outraged by Algonquin J. Calhoun, the only crooked lawyer ever allowed to be ridiculed on radio or TV. It is regrettable that this ridicule should have been so select, but then one can be grateful for whatever ridicule of crooked lawyers that was available, no matter how limited.

TV's Amos, Alvin Childress, defended the program in 1964, saying, "I didn't feel it harmed the Negro at all . . . Actually the series had many episodes which showed the Negro with professions and businesses like attorneys, store owners, and so on which they never had in TV or movies before . . ."

The television series repeated the scripts of the radio show from its weekly half-hour format which concentrated on Kingfish. His home life could hardly have represented an *idealization* of Negro family life.

SAPPHIRE: You ain' heard one word I said.
KINGFISH: You think dat's bad?
SAPPHIRE: What?
KINGFISH: I didn't mean dat, honey. I didn't mean it. It just slipped out.
SAPPHIRE: If dere's gonna be any slipping out you better stop loafing around dis house and slip out and find yourself a *job!*

Nag, nag, nag.

Kingfish never learned the perfect explanation for a man who loafs around the house all the time: he merely has to say he is either a writer or an actor. Of course, he knew he could always count on Amos for good advice and assistance when Sapphire kicked him out of the house for being a lazy loafer and when he had to room in with Andy.

KINGFISH: Look, Amos, could you do me two favors?
AMOS: What is dey, Kingfish?
KINGFISH: My wife likes you. Go up and talk to her and see if you can't get me back in wid her. And on your way . . . stop by Lightnin's house and give him dis baggage check. Tell him to go up to de station and pick up my suitcase and bring it up here to Andy's room.
AMOS: Okay, Kingfish. I'll take care of everything. And good luck to me on dis mess.

Naturally, it was Andy whom Kingfish dragged in on one of his devious schemes. Andy was to show Sapphire a letter from the Kingfish, supposedly from overseas. Sapphire was to think a heartbroken Kingfish had gone off to war—whichever war that happened to be going on at the time. Surely, she would welcome back a wounded veteran in a few weeks.

ANDY: You got de letter all writ, Kingfish?
KINGFISH: Yeah. See how dis sound: "Dear Andy: Just a line to tell you I has done arrived at de front . . ."
ANDY: Hey, Kingfish, look at dat inkspot you got on de paper dere. Can't you rub dat out?
KINGFISH: I put dat blot dere on purpose. You see I switches to writin' in pencil here . . . "Andy, please 'scuse de rest of this being writ in pencil, but my fountain pen was just shot outta my hand."

Kingfish's scheme failed as usual, but Sapphire took him back anyway. Amos's little talk with her probably filled her with Christian charity.

It was Amos who expressed in simple but effective language the basic decency of both himself and of Andy and of Freeman Gosden and Charles Correll. In the traditional *Amos 'n' Andy* Christmas program, broadcast for many years, he explained to his daughter Arbadella the meaning of the Lord's Prayer on Christmas Eve.

AMOS: . . . "Thy Kingdom come, Thy will be done in Earth as it is in Heaven . . ." that means as we clean our hearts of all hate and selfishness and fill our hearts with love—the good, the true, and the beautiful—then this earth where we is now will be just like Heaven . . . "Give us this day our daily bread . . ." that means, honey, to feed our hearts and minds with kindness and love and courage which make us strong . . . "Forgive us our debts as we forgive our debtors . . . For Thyne is the Kingdom, and the Power, and the Glory forever . . . Ahmen . . ." that means that all the world and everything in it belongs to God's Kingdom—your mommy, your daddy, your grandmother, your uncle Andy—you and everybody— And as we know that and act as if we do know it, that, my dear daughter, is the real spirit of Christmas . . ."

Both Amos and Andy had a certain innate innocence for they were in reality those universal human character types, the back-country provincials who come to the big city and find themselves in conflict with the ways of that city. The dialect was incidental. They might have been immigrant German "Dutch," or Russian "Yids," or Tennessee hillbillies. Because of the minstrel show background of their creators, they were cast as Negroes. In reality, Amos and Andy were all of us, reluctantly leaving the rural unsophistication of the first half of the twentieth century for our inevitable trip into the urban mechanization of the second half of the century.

As we traveled farther into awareness, we left behind *Amos 'n' Andy*. Theirs was a time when everybody in America, rich or poor, black or white, was too innocent not to love Amos 'n' Andy.

6.

When Teen-agers Were Kids

MOTHER (*calling*): Henry! Henry Aldrich!
HENRY: Com-ming, mother!

So began *The Aldrich Family*, radio's most popular situation comedy about teen-agers.

The introduction to the program itself explained much of its appeal. "A typical teen-age boy like Henry Aldrich," announcer Day Seymour explained, "lives in a world all his own—a world of impulses, hectic activity, and honest enthusiasms; and grown-ups always welcome the opportunity to re-enter that wonderful world."

HENRY: Boy, Homer sure wanted a new band for his watch . . . But a present for the anniversary of his first meeting with Agnes came first . . . If I had a little more money, I'd buy him that watchband myself.

FATHER: I'll tell you what, Henry. Since it's Homer's . . . "anniversary," I'll match whatever you put up. How much do you have in your dime bank?

HENRY: A dime.

FATHER: Well, that gives us twenty cents.

MOTHER: I'll match what *both* of you put up.

FATHER: Forty cents. How much more . . .

HENRY: About sixty . . .

MOTHER: The milk bottles! Henry, there are five empty ones on the back porch.

HENRY: That's another quarter . . .

FATHER: Maybe if we looked under the sofa cushions . . .

HENRY: Sure!

MOTHER: My cushions!

HENRY: A dime. I found a dime.

FATHER: There's something shiny over there—

HENRY: Another di— Father, did you lose a suspender button?

MOTHER: There's a nickel . . .

HENRY: Boy, at this rate, my troubles will soon be over.

Henry Aldrich was *always* in trouble. The announcer's phrase after the middle commercial was entirely apt: "And now, back to the troubles of Henry Aldrich . . ." Not "adventures," not "escapades," but "troubles." Henry always dropped his father's suit in a street being paved with hot tar en route to the cleaners. He always found out at the last minute that he did not have enough cash in hand to take his girl to the big dance, and was in trouble. He tried to make the football team by exercising through the methods in a book of Yoga he found and sprained his back. Wherever Henry went, trouble was soon to follow.

It was hilarious listening to Henry Aldrich when you were a kid not a whole lot younger than he was. Henry was the only guy we knew who was constantly in more trouble than we were. What a creep! He made us seem as self-sufficient as

Clark Gable or Gary Cooper. You couldn't help liking a kid like that.

Certainly Henry was likable. He inspired dogged dedication in his best friend, Homer Brown. His parents, Sam and Alice Aldrich, really probably liked him best, even though they had a saccharine-sweet daughter, Mary. His teachers and the athletic coach recognized in him the problem child, but liked and tried to help him.

Yet despite all that help and good will, Henry eternally seemed to get himself trapped into some humiliating situation or other by his utter refusal to do the logical thing and to tell the truth about what was going wrong, admitting his own boyish blunders.

He would not admit to either of the two girls whom he invited to the prom that through simple human emotion, on a moonlit spring night, he had invited one girl too many. He would not admit to his even more inept friend, Homer, that he, Henry, knew no more about handling women than Homer did, and that his advice was less than useless on how Homer could relieve his girl friend, Agnes's, misconception that Homer had proposed marriage to her.

Henry was so overwhelmed by the process of growing up that he could not even admit to his own sister, Mary, that he had knocked over a box of chocolates sent her by a boy friend. As he reached into the family closet, he had sent the chocolates flying into his aunt's umbrella, his father's shoes, and all over the floor. Good old Homer was there to help Henry pick up the candy to get it out of sight before Mary or another member of the family could find out about the mishap. For Homer, one excellent hiding place was his own stomach.

HENRY: We'd better hide the chocolates here in the fruit dish . . . Don't wipe your hands on the tablecloth, Homer.

HOMER: I'm not. I'm just . . . feeling to see what kind of material
    it is . . .

MR. ALDRICH (*coming on*): Homer, what's that you have on your
    hands?

HOMER: Why, why—boy, they look just like I'd been in a mud-
    puddle, don't they?

MR. ALDRICH: You'd better go upstairs and wash them.

HOMER: Yes, Mr. Aldrich. Come on, Hen . . .

MARY: Father, what are you limping for?

MR. ALDRICH: Limping? Oh, there seems to be something wrong
    with one of my shoes . . . I had this pair in the hall closet, and
    it may be my imagination, but I think there's something down
    in the toe of one.

MARY: Really? Why don't you take it out?

MR. ALDRICH: Oh, it's probably just the lining, or something. It's
    soft and it gives when I walk.

Obviously, Henry's troubles were just beginning. When
Henry's aunt opened that umbrella of hers and felt a rain of
mashed chocolates coming down on her, there would be a few
words for Henry.

With a cracking whine, Henry would often admit, "I'm
worried, Homer!" Homer would always try to bumble out
something encouraging, but in the final instance, anyone
would have to admit that Henry had plenty of good reasons
to be worried. He could never have posed for the grinning,
carefree simpleton that is mascot to *Mad Magazine*. Henry's
motto was *not* "What—me worry?"

Like most twentieth-century males, Henry was hopelessly brow-beaten and henpecked by women even before
marriage. His mother told him what to do, his teacher told
him what to do, his girl friend told him what to do (and
sometimes he was even pushed around by Homer's girl,
Agnes).

Henry Aldrich was even a bit leery of his sister, who was older than he. More than once she gave Henry her opinion of him and his little "playmates." Yet Mary may have been the one female in his life that Henry could get back at in even the smallest way. A sister was just a sister, but the shortages of World War II proved that a new baseball was a boy's best friend.

MARY: But Henry, don't you see my point of view—you had no right to do a thing like that.

HENRY: But Mary, Charlie Clark is a nice guy—he's really a swell guy—he's really very good-looking.

MARY: How can you tell? His hair is always falling down in front of his face.

HENRY: Not at night it isn't. When he goes out at night, he has some stuff he puts on his hair that—Boy—it makes it stiff as a board.

MARY: Let me warn you, Henry, if Charlie Clark comes over here tonight I won't even see him.

HENRY: Why not?

MARY: Because you had no right to make such a date for me.

MRS. ALDRICH: Mary, is it necessary for you and Henry to talk quite so loud?

MARY: Mother, I'm not talking loud. But do you know what Henry did to me? Do you know what he did?

MRS. ALDRICH: What did he do?

MARY: He sold me to Charlie Clark for a baseball!

HENRY: Mother, I assure you the baseball had nothing to do with it. Besides, Mary, do you realize how hard a thing like that is to get these days?

Henry's moment of mutiny against the females in the family was short-lived. His mother saw to it that Henry set things right with Charlie about the baseball.

92 The Great Radio Comedians

Yet, the Aldrich house was not matriarchal in design, just in its casual everyday execution. Sam Aldrich was really the head of his family and exercised a stern but kindly command of it. He recognized that Henry had his troubles, and he was sympathetic. Sam Aldrich could not really be said to be perplexed or confused by Henry's behavior. He had gone through much the same thing himself, and the only confusion there was resulted from hazy memory.

The generation gap was far less wide in those days. The life Henry Aldrich was leading in the forties was not much different from the one his father had lead in the twenties. There was still the same round of familiar things of the teen-agers' life: rumble seats, dance bands, and the Senior Prom.

Just as the kids in the audience felt that they had *almost* as many problems as Henry, or had a brother or a chum who was "just like" him, the fathers listening in could remember living through many of the same kinds of experiences as Henry was having.

The problems for fathers and sons had been similar: whether or not to have another chocolate soda for fear of what it might do to the complexion; whether to take your girl to a Western movie you wanted to see, or to a romantic one she wanted to see (and which might put her in the mood for a little smooching).

Who could imagine that their sons and grandsons would worry about whether or not to smoke marijuana, and that their Saturday matinees would resemble the sights and sounds of a Far Eastern orgy?

The original author of *The Aldrich Family*, Clifford Goldsmith, wrote a playlet comparing Henry's era with ours today for a special live Hollywood Bowl presentation in 1968, *Frank DeVol's Great Old Days of Radio*. In the 1940s,

Henry timorously asked his father for the loan of the car. In the 1960s, the same son *told* his cowed father when he would be through with the car and when the old man could have it. Henry was going out with the other teen-agers on important business: to decide which teachers they would allow to remain in school. "Have a nice riot," Sam Aldrich called after his boy.

Today's parents are no longer amused by the hectic activities of their children. The kids, in turn, would be aghast by Henry's respect for parental authority. Would Henry Aldrich be accepted today? "Only as a museum piece," sighed Ezra Stone, who played the part of Henry for some fifteen years.

Stone first played the role during times which were far less free and easy than today's. In the Depression year of 1937, Clifford Goldsmith, already an outstanding American playwright, wrote a play called *What a Life,* produced on Broadway by George Abbott. Although only in his teens, Ezra Stone was both an assistant to Abbott in production and an actor, as well. He had played youthful parts in *Three Men on a Horse* and *Brother Rat* to excellent reviews. But Abbott murmured darkly that he was not right for the part of Henry Aldrich, a high school student who was always in trouble with the superintendent.

In his capacity of production assistant, Stone read the part in try-outs with other actors. For Henry, he used an imitation he did of a one-time schoolmate of his whose voice cracked under the slightest stress. Once before, Stone had used this voice for the part of a telegraph delivery boy in a nameless sketch performed in the Catskill Mountains. It worked well in the part of Henry Aldrich. Producer Abbott listened attentively to Stone running through the rehearsals, but he seemed to prefer another young actor, Eddie Bracken, for the part.

Finally, Abbott admitted Stone was being considered along with Bracken for the role. The two young men were told to come back to the office in one hour for the decision from Olympus. When they returned, Mr. Abbott's secretary got up from her chair and handed Stone a single red rose.

Eventually, Ezra Stone was given starring credit on the marquee. Unfortunately, the Biltmore Theatre had no letter "Z" to use on its two electric light signs. With an inventiveness that paled Henry Aldrich's own, Stone borrowed two "Z's" from a nearby motion picture house which was showing Paul Muni in *The Life of Emile Zola*.

The first appearance of the Aldrich Family on radio came on the Rudy Vallee show the same year the play was on Broadway. It was such a smash success that the advertising agency for the Vallee Show began negotiations for a regular scheduling of the Aldriches with Vallee. But at the last moment, the agency was outbid by the representatives of *The Kate Smith Hour*. The "Songbird of the South" had Ezra Stone and company doing an eight-minute sketch on her show for a full year, along with the comedy team of Bud Abbott and Lou Costello, and the mock-quiz, *It Pays to Be Ignorant*, both of which, like *The Aldrich Family*, soon became half-hour regular shows of their own.

Goldsmith continued to write the weekly adventures of Henry Aldrich, although he once said, "After writing a three-act play about the kid, what more can I say about him?" He drew so much on his experiences with his own children that they once threatened, jokingly, to sue him for plagiarism. The playwright always maintained a gentle balance between outright comedy and the bittersweet problems of growing up. In later years, a staff of writers including Norman Tokar,

Frank Tarloff, and Ed Jurist took over for Goldsmith, and the farce became much broader. (Goldsmith himself still writes other situation comedies for TV.)

Goldsmith and his successors had a nearly ideal cast to perform their scripts. Besides Ezra Stone, there was the head of the Aldrich clan, Sam, played by House Jameson, who came from the stage to radio in 1935, playing many famous roles, including *Renfrew of the Mounted*.

House Jameson not only sounded the part of wise, kindly Sam Aldrich—he looked it: tall, distinguished, handsome as an eagle. He shared the quality of living up to his looks with Jackie Kelk, who played Homer Brown. Although some years older than high school age, Kelk looked youthful enough to be still going to classes. On radio, with a slightly lower and less comic voice, he played both young Terry on *Terry and the Pirates* and cub reporter Jimmy Olson on *Superman* at various times. On television, he joined Jameson in playing their original *Aldrich Family* roles on the home screen in the fifties.

Unfortunately, Ezra Stone was then undeniably too mature to play Henry Aldrich visually; he had served a long hitch in the Army during World War II. While he was away at war, from 1941 to 1944, various actors filled in for him as Henry on radio, including one of the writers, Norman Tokar. On TV, Henry was played by Dick Tyler and others. The role turned over rapidly, since "Henry" kept being drafted for the Korean War.

Katherine Raht and Mary Shipp played Mrs. Aldrich and Mary on radio; various other ladies took the roles on television.

Stone continued to act the part of Henry on the radio, while he served as director of the TV series. During this period, the NBC studios were still crowded with big nighttime radio shows, so much so that dressing room space was at a premium. Ezra Stone shared his dressing room with Jo Stafford, songstress of the *Supper Club*. They used the same cubbyhole during periods several hours apart and seldom ever met, even in passing. However, Stone's mother was taken aback one evening to open his dressing room closet and find it filled with frilly frocks and lacy dressing gowns. He had to explain hastily that he, a respectable married man, was not entertaining young ladies in his quarters.

Women seemed to be crowding Stone in more ways than one in radio.

In fact, most of the other comedy shows about teen-agers had a girl—not a boy like Henry—as their central character. There were highly imitative series about *Archie Andrews* and *That Brewster Boy* but both were relatively short-lived. The problems of adolescent girls seemed funnier to radio audiences, but then girls are allowed to be brainless and charming at any age. There were, among others, *Junior Miss*, *Meet Corliss Archer*, *Maudie's Diary*, and *A Date with Judy*.

Despite wearing skirts, Judy Foster bore a certain resemblance to Henry Aldrich.

OOGIE: Hiya, Judy! Gee, you look more beautiful in the morning before you've put on your face than most girls do at a party. You look sn-aa-zy!

JUDY: Oh, Oogie—I'm a fright! I'm even worse than that, with my face all washed. I look—I look *wholesome* . . . What's that in your hand, Oogie?

OOGIE: Oh, it's a present for you, Judy. It's a picture of something you like very much—of V.A.N.

JUDY: Of Van! Van Johnson? Why, Oogie Pringle! How could you! It's nothing but a picture of an old moving van!

OOGIE: April Fool!

JUDY: April Fool? Of all the infantile, childish goings-on . . .

OOGIE: Why—last year, Judy, you practically ruined the whole

Oogie Pringle Hot Licks Band when you smeared molasses all over the mouthpieces of the saxophone and the trombone. You weren't too old for April Fool then!

Henry Aldrich or his buddy, Homer Brown, would not have the gumption to pull that sort of a gag on one of their girl friends.

Remember that money Henry was scrounging up out of sofa cushions and old milk bottles? He took it to the jewelry store to buy that watchband for Homer. Through a stroke of fortune to which only Henry was heir, he inadvertently glanced at a tray of engagement rings in front of some of the other girls from school.

Henry and Homer found out the same thing Dexter did with Judy—girls are in deadly earnest about gifts.

AGNES (*on the telephone*): Isn't it wonderful, Homer—another wonderful, thrilling year since we first met . . . And Homer, I just want you to know I don't expect anything as an anniversary present. I have *you*. What more could any girl ask for?

HOMER: Nothing, Agnes . . .

AGNES: Homer Brown, haven't you decided on what you're going to give me?

HOMER: Sort of . . . Henry's supposed to be thinking of something.

AGNES: Give me a hint . . .

HOMER: I can't. Henry said you'd try to force it out of me, so he wouldn't even tell *me* . . .

AGNES: I think I know . . .

HOMER: Gee, everybody knows what I'm giving you but me . . . What *am* I giving you?

AGNES: I don't think I should tell you—it'll spoil the surprise.

HOMER: Listen, Agnes . . . *you're* supposed to be surprised.

AGNES: Okay, Homer, come on over—I want to see your face . . .

when you give me that engagement ring ... (*Hangs up phone*)

HOMER: I never thought of Agnes as something to get engaged to ... Engaged! Henry, Mr. Bradley will throw me out of school!

HENRY: See? I told you there were advantages to being engaged!

Time was running out for Henry Aldrich and for radio in the early fifties, and Ezra Stone wisely got out. Today, he is a busy director, making industrial films and directing such television situation comedies as *The Flying Nun* and *Julia*.

The nature of Henry Aldrich's problems are hard for us to fully appreciate today and impossible for the new generation of teens to relate to (in our time, what teen-ager would be worrying about raising a single dollar to buy a gift for his girl friend?). Henry Aldrich, Frank Merriwell, Jack Armstrong have all had to face up to the fact that the day of the All-American Boy has been replaced by the era of the uni-sex look in fashions.

7.

Sidekicks

"Honest to my Grandma, Jack . . ."

"Sufferin' snakes—the Har-nut!"

"Jumpin-jiminy-gee-whiz, Uncle Jim . . ."

These comedy lines were almost as famous in radio as those belonging to higher-budgeted comedians, including "Jell-O, again!" and "Wanna buy a duck?"

The laughable sidekick carried the humor in dramatized radio. In the world of the thirties, the hero always seemed to remain true to stereotyped form. Even in those days, Jack Armstrong seemed to be concerned with his "image." He would never crack a joke or a wind-chapped lip in a smile. The jokester in the group of adventurers was certainly Jack's best friend, Billy Fairfield. He corresponded to the "fun-loving" one of the Rover Boys. The tradition of high school humor is a long one.

No situation was ever too desperate for Billy to try to

relieve the tension with a breezy remark. During the basket-ball game that could win Hudson High the championship, Jack Armstrong scored basket after basket even though he was playing on an injured leg (the ankle was at the very least strained, and probably broken). "Attaboy, Jack, keep laying all those eggs in the same basket!" Even if it was just another chicken joke, Billy did his best. After all, he was just a kid, and in all charity, not too bright.

When rich Uncle Jim Fairfield came to town and pied-pipered Billy and Betty and their young leader, Jack Arm-strong, off on some mission to the jungles of South America or Africa, it was Billy who gave his serious friend the time-honored advice about head-hunters: "Let's not lose our heads, Jack."

On another occasion, the group of adventurers took the yacht, the *Walkaway*, instead of Uncle Jim's great amphibian, the *Silver Albatros*. Trouble pursued them. Aboard the *Walkaway* were a group of mutineers headed by the sailor called Fishface. No sooner had Jack shot Fishface's gun out of his hand, and locked him and his malcontents in quarters below deck, than the ship was threatened by a gigantic waterspout towering as high as the Empire State Building, powered by winds of typhoon intensity. It hardly looked as if things could get darker for our friends, but then the waterspout broke in two, spinning off a second spout which danced around the yacht. The two waterspouts seemed about to come together and crush the small ship between them. In this case, Billy's lighthearted remarks must have been carried away with the wind, but the announcer filled in for him with a classic understatement: "Say, being caught between two waterspouts is dangerous business."

Sometimes there was adventure closer to home. Hudson, U.S.A., had to be somewhere in the Midwest and Jack and

13. Amos 'n' Andy in make-up for their 1930 movie, *Check and Double Check,* go on with their regular NBC broadcast between filming scenes, according to this publicity shot.

14. Without make-up, Freeman Gosden (Amos) and Charles Correll (Andy) mug for their 1950 radio series, *The Amos 'n' Andy Music Hall.*

15. Dick York tries to fit his big feet into Japanese sandals. The scene was for the 1955 movie, *Sergeant O'Reilly*, but was typical of the troubles he had got into some six years before on radio as Jack Armstrong's trouble-prone buddy, Billy Fairfield.

16. Bing Crosby and Bob Hope were still entertaining the troops on NBC radio just after World War II.

17. Hope and Crosby with a hairy friend in some of the zaniness from the 1952 movie, *Road to Bali*. The *Road* pictures were constantly being borrowed from for sketches on the Hope and Crosby radio shows.

18. Bob Burns, the bazooka-playing comedian of the *Kraft Music Hall* and later his own show, pores over fan mail with his wife at his Bel-Air home in 1937.

19. Jimmy Durante started out in vaudeville but successfully moved into radio when he teamed with the *Club Matinee* comedian, Garry Moore. Subsequently, they both gained their own series.

20. Michael Rafetto, Gloria Blondell (Joan's sister), Barbara Jean Wong and Barton Yarborough of *I Love a Mystery* pose for the CBS cameraman in 1943. Barton Yarborough was a fine light comedian who often was the archtypical Texan for Jack Benny and other stars. He was most famous, however, as Doc Long (shown here), the comic sidekick to Rafetto's Jack Packard.

21. Eddie Cantor and Al Jolson, two great performers equally gifted in comedy and song. Taken April 15, 1937, at the CBS radio studios.

22. Jack Benny's ancient Maxwell, one of the most famous (but generally unseen) props in radio, is examined by Benny and a great performer, Eddie "Rochester" Anderson.

23. Here are more of the perfect comedy cast of *The Jack Benny Show* in 1950 (from left to right): announcer Don Wilson, Mary Livingstone, Jack, and the forever naïve boy singer, Dennis Day.

24. "Archie Himself" Ed Gardner sports his *Duffy's Tavern* apron with the autographs of some of the celebrities who had put a few down in the legendary saloon.

25. Fred Allen and his zany crew set out on the dry sea of comedy. The shipmates for the "Texaco Star Theater" series during the mid-forties comprised comedienne Portland Hoffa, bandleader Al Goodman, Minerva Pious (Mrs. Nussbaum), Allen himself, Charlie Cantor (later "Finnegan" of *Duffy's Tavern*), tenor Kenny Baker, announcer Jimmy Wallington.

his friends occasionally got to Chicago where they naturally ran into gangsters. In the wartime year of 1943 the gangsters Jack Armstrong encountered were counterfeiting ration coupons. For once these mobsters did not have Italian names. The two chief rivals in the business of bootlegging ration stamps were the Black Vulture and the Silencer.

Jack and Billy were crawling through high grass near a supposedly abandoned roadhouse nightclub to spy on the rival gangland chiefs.

BILLY: Doggone those mosquitoes!

JACK: Be quiet, Billy. Our lives depend on it . . .

BILLY: I'm trying to be quiet, but that mosquito bit me . . . Boy, why do I get myself into situations like this?

JACK: Freeze, Billy, that crook is throwing his light over this way.

BILLY: I couldn't move if I wanted to. My belt's hooked on a piece of bailing wire . . . (Help me get it loose . . .) Now let's make a run for it.

JACK: No, Billy—let's get inside that door . . .

BILLY: Shall I close the door, Jack?

JACK (*patiently*): Yes, Billy . . . If you hear anyone coming, get back on top of that chandelier (where we hid before) . . .

BILLY: I feel like a monkey sitting up there.

JACK: That doesn't make any difference, Billy . . .

It is interesting to note that the actor who played Billy, Dick York, has for years been outsmarted on the air, in television's *Bewitched* and by his TV wife, Elizabeth Montgomery. Michael Rye, who played Jack (following Jim Ameche and Charles Flynn), is still equally infallible as the voice of TV's animated cartoon Lone Ranger.

Another of radio's afternoon serial heroes, Tom Mix, had not just one comic sidekick, but a whole posse of them.

Among Tom Mix's Straight Shooters were Pecos, a drawling, semi-hillbilly cowpoke; Sheriff Mike Shaw, a gruff but lovable law man given to exclaiming "Texas Ticks and Tumbleweeds!"; Wrangler, a story-spinning, mustache-chewing foreman; and Wash, the cook and "man-of-all-work" who was a Negro and who spoke a dialect fully as authentic as that of the Westerners on the TM-Bar Ranch. Only the children on the ranch, Jimmy and Jane, had some of the same stern maturity that Tom Mix projected.

The more genuinely funny of Tom Mix's sidekicks was undoubtedly Wash (short for Washington Jefferson Lincoln Lee), played by a fine comedian, Forrest Lewis. Lewis, formerly a "blackface" comic in some of the last of the minstrel stage shows, has gone on to co-star in such Walt Disney films as *The Absent Minded Professor*. But it was as Wash played to Curley Bradley as Tom Mix that he is unforgettable to two generations of grownup boys and girls.

While Wash was saddled with many of the stereotype characteristics of the Negro in his era of 1933 to 1950, he always seemed to rise above these limitations. Wash was afraid of ghosts. Yet when the Straight Shooters were searching for the lost treasure of the Golden God of the Toltecs and were confronted by knife-wielding "ghosts" of the centuries-dead Toltec priests, Wash was understandably upset, but his first thought was not entirely of himself: "Yowww— lemme outa here! I'll save yo', Miss Jane!" Wash tucked Jane under one arm and beat a retreat from the armed band. Tom Mix himself could not be of help because he had been sealed in an ancient tomb with skeletons and golden plunder to die of suffocation by a renegade archaeologist who wanted the treasure all for himself. Later, it was Jane and Wash who lead the real Indians against the phony ones and helped rescue Tom. Wash echoed the sentiment of all heroes: "Dis am agin my rejudgment—but ah suppose ah gotta be brave too . . ."

Like many of the leading personalities of the day, from Babe Ruth to real-life G-man Melvin Purvis, Wash also gave commercial endorsements—memorable ones.

ANNOUNCER: There's one sure cure for those winter morning shivers and shakes, and that's a steaming bowl of good old Instant Ralston Wheat Cereal.

WASH: Um-hmmm, Mist' Don Gordon, you said it that time. Instant Ralston Wheat Cereal warm you up from head to toe, just as quick as a wunk—wonk—I mean *wink*. Why, just the thought of that golden brown, mouth-watering, tasty, scrambunctious, delicious, hypersnortive cereal just a-steaming in the dish all nice and hot, just the thought of it makes me perspire with pleasure . . .

ANNOUNCER: Remember—your best bet for a winter-time breakfast is—

WASH: Good old lovable, super-cataclysmic Instant Ralston—the most mouth-watering name in the English language . . . Instant Ralston—that's all you got to say and you gonna get the best breakfast your taster ever tasted!

Wash was an example of a writer being saddled with a faulty concept that had outlived whatever usefulness it may have had. Scripter George Lowther was given the stereotype of a comic, cowardly Negro, developed in an innocent, even ignorant day, and developed every ounce of humor and good will in the idea. Actor Lewis did his best too. Wash became lovable, heroic, ingenious. The obligatory demands of tradition—that we be reminded from time to time that he was only laughable and cowardly—were thumbs stuck in the eye of our imagination. Unlike Billy Fairfield or other sidekicks, Wash *grew*. He outgrew every limitation except a tattered character outline sheet handed down by the producer from an earlier generation.

Even radio's other great Western hero, the Lone Ranger, also had a comic sidekick, although one who was not so prominent in the show and who may not be so well-remembered. It was certainly *not* Tonto, the Masked Man's faithful Indian companion. Tonto was even sterner and more taciturn of speech than the Lone Ranger himself. The humorous sidekick did not appear in every one of the three half-hour stories a week, but perhaps in one every two weeks. He was Thunder Martin, a gruff mule-skinner with a heart of gold (or perhaps in deference to his masked friend's famous bullets, a heart of pure silver).

Thunder Martin was sometimes funny, but he could never be described as witty. He did not display much wit—let alone, simple intelligence—when the Lone Ranger's worst enemy, Butch Cavendish, escaped jail. It was Cavendish's gang that had ambushed six Texas Rangers in Bryant's Gap, leaving all six for dead. But one single Ranger survived to become the Lone Ranger and to put all of the Cavendish gang in prison. When Cavendish broke out, seeking revenge, he went to the Hornblow ranch and asked Thunder Martin where he could find the Lone Ranger. Obligingly, Thunder told him. Later, he told of the man's visit to Tonto. In retrospect, something was troubling Thunder. "He was a big galoot, but he was wearing clothes too small for him—like he had borrowed them from somebody. And his face was all white, like he had been inside a lot." Stoically, Tonto explained to Thunder Martin that this man was an escaped convict out to kill the Lone Ranger, and that he, Tonto, had to go warn the Masked Man. (He was, thank Providence, in time.)

Thunder Martin was played by a number of actors, perhaps

most memorably by Paul Hughes, whose voice growled even deeper than that of Brace Beemer as the Lone Ranger.

After driving mules for some years, Thunder Martin finally settled down as foreman on the ranch owned by Clarabelle Hornblow, who was also gruff but lovable (at least to Thunder). Thunder and Clarabelle were such good friends of the Lone Ranger and Tonto that he entrusted them to raise the colt of his great white stallion, Silver. Years later, the colt was given to the Masked Man's nephew, Dan Reid, who named him "Victor."

In many respects, the Green Hornet was the Lone Ranger in modern dress. The Hornet's comedy relief was, however, much more prominent in the story line, appearing in almost every broadcast. Michael Axford was a former policeman hired by publisher old Dan Reid (the same Dan Reid who was the Lone Ranger's young nephew) to be a bodyguard for Reid's son, Britt. Although he seemed to prefer the life of a playboy, Britt Reid took over the office of publisher of the *Daily Sentinel* newspaper, filling the office with only intermittent efficiency. His main job came at night when he took up the mask and gas gun of the Green Hornet and rode out in his streamlined Black Beauty car with his faithful valet, Kato, to smash racketeers who hid within legal loopholes. Axford proved no help to Reid as a bodyguard or later as a reporter on the *Sentinel*. He may have meant well, but he was obviously not one to be trusted with the Hornet's secret. In his ignorance, Axford was one of Britt Reid's staunchest allies, and the Green Hornet's most implacable foe.

In one adventure, Axford took a job in a defense plant to help expose crooked gamblers who were fleecing the workers. Unfortunately, subterfuge was not one of Axford's strong points, and he was quickly spotted and locked in a backroom in the factory offices. He would be disposed of later. But the Green Hornet arrived in the nick of time, getting into a gun fight with the crooks, non-lethal gas against bullets. Two thugs went down, but a third got the drop on the masked crime fighter. This rival crook did not know that Axford was tied up in the next room.

THUMB: I'm takin' over Stevens' records! His mob too! It's all mine. I'm a loner from now on.

HORNET: You're not alone, Thumb! There's a witness next door who's heard everything!

THUMB: Maybe you want me to put down these gats an' go see? Hornet, you seen too many movies.

HORNET: You don't believe me, eh? Okay, hello there? Who's in the next room?

AXFORD: N-n-no-ooo . . . n-nobody's in . . . here . . .

THUMB: What th–? Who's in there—arrrghhh . . .

HORNET: That's all I wanted. You to turn away for an instant. This gas will keep you asleep till the police come . . .
(*FADE*)

OFFICER O'HARA: Well, for– Look! Axford of the Daily *Sentinel!* Covering three of them!

AXFORD: A' course, three of the worst spalPeens in town! When Michael Axford goes after someone, he gets them dead or alive! Go git the Green Har-nut! I'd a took him myself, only me hands was full!

Of course, Axford's hands had been untied by the Green Hornet before he buzzed off into the night.

Recently, I discussed both the Green Hornet and the Lone Ranger with their creator-producer, George W. Trendle, and with Lee Allman, who played Miss Lenore Case, Britt Reid's Girl Friday. Out of these discussions came some instances of radio humor that was not in the script.

In one such instance, the original actor to play Mike Axford was Jim Irwin, who played to Al Hodge's Britt Reid. Irwin died suddenly and an emergency replacement had to be found. The show originated in Detroit, which did not have as many actors to draw upon as Hollywood or New York. Many members of the casts of the WXYZ shows were moonlighting from other more regular positions. A Detroit businessman auditioned for the part of Axford. He had a beautiful Irish brogue, but he was not used to reading lines. The director, Jim Jewell, kept patiently asking him for *feeling,* to put more emotion into his reading. At last, the businessman worked himself up to an emotional pitch. "I hope they nab that no-good spalPeen, the Har-nut! I hope they get him! I hope they get that lousy son of a b——" He was cut off the air, and out of the part. (Finally, a full-time professional, Gil Shea, took over as Axford.)

Stupidity seemed a strong point with sidekicks in Radioland. On *Buck Rogers in the Twenty-fifth Century* this element was partially offset by a humorous partner who was extremely intelligent—Dr. Huer. Edgar Stehli as Huer was not even an *absent-minded* professor. He could remember everything. The humor came often from his excruciatingly exact description of some scientific gadget on the spaceship piloted by Buck Rogers. "What is that device you are working on?" beautiful Wilma Deering might inquire. Dr. Huer's response went something like: "Why, Wilma, this is an Intergalactic Stellar Radiational Environmental Computer Analysis Regulator-Detector Calibrator Data Ingestational Auditory-Visual Response Simulator Recorder-Projector." That meant, in short, it was a gadget to see whether the stars were shining outside.

However, even in the educated world of science, or at least, science fiction, there was no final escape from the dim-witted sidekick. On the *Buck Rogers* radio show, the dull-edged associate was Black Barney, a reformed space pirate who became a right-hand man to Captain Buck Rogers and the forces of law and order in outer space. Joe Granby as Barney carried on conversations with Curtis Arnall as Buck that went like this.

BUCK: Buck Rogers calling Black Barney . . .

BARNEY: Hello, Captain Rogers—how are you? . . . Why I haven't heard from you since we got thru exploring under the Earth. I understand you're looking for Killer Kane and Ardala?

BUCK: Right. Have you seen any sign of them?

BARNEY: Captain, with them crooks on the loose, the minute I got back here to Mars I got everything all organized and fixed up a fleet of Space Patrols, and just yesterday one of the pilots saw a strange super-rocketship heading towards a little plasteroid—

BUCK: You mean "planetoid."

BARNEY: Yeah, plasteroid that lays fourteen points west of here in the same orbit as Mars has. With his teleradioscope in sharp focus, the pilot could see it was Killer Kane heading right for Saturn.

BUCK: Great. So you sent patrol ships out after it?

BARNEY: Captain—uh—in getting things all organized out in such a hurry, I forgot to equip my patrol ships with rocket guns or— or anything . . .

In this sequence from the mid-1930s and the rest of the series, Black Barney was certainly done an injustice in comparison to his image in the original *Buck Rogers* comic strip by Phil Nowland and Dick Calkins. In this first incarnation, Black Barney may well have been the *most clever* of all the characters in the story. He was a bit coarse of speech, but he was shrewd. In the beginning, he seemed always trying to work some angle of his own, perhaps ready to go over to the side of the villainous Killer Kane if it was to his own advantage, but he certainly was not stupid. In time, he actually became the *leader* of the good guys when Buck himself was away, as he was for months at a time. Radio, like television, was often accused of making an adaptation from another medium that turned out pretty dumb. Black Barney may have been the dumbest adaptation of all.

In another series—in the greatest adventure serial of them all—the good-natured sidekick probably only appeared dumb in contrast to his serious, logical partner. Doc Long was not really a dumb, back-country Texas boy, although he sometimes appeared to be just that in comparison to Jack Packard on *I Love a Mystery*. There was no suggestion of ignorance in their cultured English partner, Reggie York, although there was at times fun with his youthful innocence and overly formal manners.

Carlton E. Morse, one of the finest writers in broadcasting, created the series especially for radio. Its three heroes were based to some degree on the personalities of the first three actors to play Jack, Doc and Reggie—Michael Rafetto, Barton Yarborough, and Walter Patterson. Later the program was revived with a new cast—Russell Thorson, Jim Boles, and Tony Randall. In playing Doc Long in this second series, Jim Boles was only giving an expert imitation of the natural speech and personality of Barton Yarborough, the model Doc.

Doc Long retained his sense of humor through countless adventures with master criminals, spies, werewolves, vampires, beautiful girls, gangsters, and crazed cowboys. In one story, Jack and Doc were tricked into getting into the prizefight ring with two gigantic professional boxers who allegedly were able to effortlessly maim for life the two friends. Just

to make a more colorful show for an eccentric rancher, Jack
and Doc were going to fight the other two at the same time,
four men in the ring at once, while Reggie served as their
trainer in the corner.

DOC: You know somethin', son, the nearer it gets time to go in
     that ring and mop up, the better I like it.

JACK: First thing you know you'll be *enjoying* yourself.

REGGIE: ˙I think he's doing that right now.

DOC: 'Course I am. The only thing though, Jack . . . Us fighting
     double the way we're a-gonna ain't so good. . . . The fightin's
     all right . . . It's just that I got to divide the glory with you
     afterward.

JACK: That's all right with me. You are welcome to all the glory
     you can get out of *this*.

DOC: Well, that's pretty durned swell of you. Only you know
     I won't take more than my *share*.

JACK: Oh, no?

DOC: Well, I *won't*. Dad-blame it, when did I ever take more than
     my share of *anything*?

REGGIE: How about the girls?

DOC: Oh, gals is *different* . . .

Gals might be different, but Doc Long was always the
same down a long road of glorious adventure. Good-natured
and easygoing, but smart and tough enough when the chips
were down.

Doc differed from the usual stereotype in radio serials of
the inflexible hero and the useless clown partner. Human
beings are not so compartmentalized—heroes take pratfalls
and clowns know moments of passion. But in the days of
radio listening perhaps we wanted to believe for at least
fifteen minutes at a time that we never made a mistake, and
it was only our friends who made stupid blunders.

The relationship between the hero and his stooge, at least, was everywhere in radio—a foil for every shining Excalibur. There was Little Orphan Annie's Joe Corntassel; Captain Midnight's Ichabod Mudd; Superman's Jimmy Olson; Hop Harrigan's Tank Tinker; Straight Arrow's Packy; Sky King's Jim Bell; and Bobby Benson's Windy Wales (played by Don Knotts). They all had a lot of courage, including the courage to deliver a lot of lines that were only disputably funny. Such courage may be the final test of *all* comedians, whether as minor as these or the greatest of all.

8.

Murder Is No Joke

The wittiest, most urbane detective on radio was no detective, not really, but an outlaw—the Robin Hood of Modern Crime, *The Saint*.

Life itself was something of a good joke to The Saint. It was natural that his mysteries, like many of the mystery dramas of radio, would be liberally loaded with humor.

While Simon Templar, the man with the ironic halo, was capable of delivering his own punch lines, he, too, had a "buddy." His name was Hoppy.

In an adventure called "The Miracle Tea Party," The Saint and Hoppy had to listen to a radio show in order to catch a secret code message being sent out by enemy agents. The "commercial" they heard was a beautiful parody of the commercials on real radio programs, including *The Saint*.

ANNOUNCER: Is your dinner chummy with your tummy? If not— try Miracle Tea . . . This amazing tea is guaranteed not only

to relieve indigestion immediately, but to effect a complete
and permanent cure. Listen to these testimonials: Tonight,
Mr. Robinson of Palo Alto writes that Miracle Tea does everything we claim . . . Tonight Mr. Schwarts of Berkeley tells
how Miracle Tea has made a new man of him . . . And
tonight, Mrs. O'Brien of Oakland tells of her amazing cure by
Miracle Tea . . .

SAINT: The magic names—Robinson, Schwarts, and O'Brien . . .
I've got it!

HOPPY: Dis is a pretty corny program if you ask me. Why don't
you get a mystery program?

SAINT: Turn off the radio, Hoppy . . . It's so simple—beautifully
and gorgeously simple . . . It's a code. Don't you see? The
one thing I couldn't figure out was how Dr. Yee's agents knew
just when to visit the drug store. The names of those peculiar
under-the-counter packets of Miracle Tea and the names we
heard on the radio just now are the same . . .

With that deduction, Simon Templar and his simple-simon
buddy went to capture the insidious Dr. Yee.

Everybody always seemed to be doing good deeds during
World War II. The Dragon Lady turned from piracy on the
high seas to killing Japanese invaders in *Terry and the
Pirates*. I suppose Simon Templar felt he had to give up
master jewel thefts for the duration to aid the war effort by
nabbing a few spies.

Certainly author Leslie Charteris should have known exactly what his character, The Saint, would do, because as
many people have pointed out, Leslie Charteris *is* The
Saint. Every author is to some extent each of his own
creations, but Charteris bears much more of a one-to-one
relationship with his laughing modern buccaneer than most
authors do to their most celebrated characters. Charteris was
born in the Orient and grew up learning how to fight off
bandits and outwit black market swindlers; he hasn't for-

gotten. The only crimes he commits are in his imagination, of course—for which the FBI and the British CID should be grateful.

Of a long list of good to fine actors who in effect impersonated Charteris as The Saint on radio—including Edgar Barrier, Vincent Price, Barry Sullivan, and Tom Conway—Mr. Charteris recently confided to me that he feels the witty and charming Brian Aherne was "the best."

Strangely enough, the author of possibly the foremost outlaw of fiction also wrote the radio exploits of the greatest detective of them all, Sir Arthur Conan Doyle's Sherlock Holmes. Leslie Charteris wrote over forty Holmes radio plays under the pseudonym of "Bruce Taylor" and in collaboration with the fine character actor and author, Dennis Green. (Later, Mr. Green collaborated with Anthony Boucher on the series.)

The stories of Baker Street always carried an undercurrent of humor. Though a man of average wit, Dr. Watson often appeared a clown at the expensive of the razor-witted and razor-beaked detective, Holmes. As incomparably portrayed on radio as well as on the screen by Basil Rathbone and Nigel Bruce, Watson was always made the butt of Holmes's practical jokes, in which the good doctor was startled out of his remaining wits by Holmes turning up in some new disguise—as a scullery maid or an umbrella stand. It has been said, *incorrectly,* that Watson himself never revealed the faintest glimmer of a sense of humor. However, as Christopher Morley pointed out in his preface to *The Complete Sherlock Holmes,* in one instance the doctor caught his celebrated friend off guard with a jab in *The Valley of Fear.* Dr. Watson is telling Holmes that he knows full well who Professor Moriarty is. "The famous scientific criminal as famous among crooks as—" Holmes interrupts him with atypical modesty. "My blushes, Watson!" But Watson continues unruffled. "I was about to say . . . as he is unknown to the public." All in all, even Holmes had to admit that this put-down had "a distinct touch."

The shadow of the famous profile of Sherlock Holmes has cast itself across the generations, shading many famous later detectives with its outline. On the most apparent physical level, many are the great detectives who have the same hawk-like face as Holmes. The newspaper comic pages display the ultimate caricature, *Dick Tracy,* and the old pulp magazines of the thirties and radio of the same era had their own angular profile in *The Shadow.*

Primarily developed by writer Walter Gibson, The Shadow always knew what evil lurked in the hearts of men. At times he seemed innocent of the wiles of women. His friendly companion, Margo Lane, always seemed to be able to lure him into quaint little pink tea shoppes against his better judgment.

In one such little out of the way place—actually a cozy French restaurant—The Shadow, in his guise of Lamont Cranston, wealthy man about town, learned from the owner, Suzette, of a smuggling ring that was allegedly getting illegal aliens into the country, including one of Suzette's relations. Except the Frenchman had mysteriously disappeared.

Without hardly more than a bowl of onion soup for sustenance, Cranston was off for the "European" city of Lucarto, with Margo in tow.

En route to the airport, Cranston's personal hackie, Shrevie, must have inquired "Should I come along, Mr. Cranston, hey, so's that I can bang a few of the proper heads for you, hey?" But Cranston told Shrevie to stay

behind. (Shrevie was one dumb sidekick who never played
too large a part in the stories. Cranston probably did not
want to pay his airlines fare, and Shrevie was not adept
enough at making change, unlike some cabbies, so he could
not pay his own way.)

In Lucarto, Cranston assumed the pose of a French refugee
who wanted in to the United States. However, just as the
Pope is only infallible under certain specific conditions (he
may be courteously corrected if he mistakes a bluejay for a
robin in his garden), Cranston was only infallible as The
Shadow. As Cranston, he goofed up the French disguise and
almost got himself and Margo killed.

It was time for The Shadow, and there would be no
kidding about it. Some fictional creations can stand self-
parody, but The Shadow cannot stand being made light of
—he belongs to the darkness of mystery and fear. The Shadow
so terrified the final smuggler in the gang that he jumped
out of an airplane just to get away from that haunting
laugh.

With fun and games over, Lamont and Margo returned to
Suzette's State-side cafe.

MARGO: I'm certainly glad to be back home, Lamont. We had
    some narrow escapes on that one.
CRANSTON: Yes, but it was worth it, Margo. The evidence we
    were able to turn over to the authorities will help smash that
    alien smuggling ring once and for all . . . Here comes
    Suzette . . .
SUZETTE: Ah, my friends, you have earned my gratitude . . .
MARGO: You did a real service, Suzette, in helping Mr. Cranston
    break up that smuggling ring . . .
SUZETTE: Now, what can I bring you from the menu?
CRANSTON: No, no, you don't catch me that easily. I'm not ordering
    from a *French* menu any more.

SUZETTE: But why?

CRANSTON: After what happened to me in Lucarto because of my French accent—from now on, I'm adhering strictly to *ham and eggs!*

The Shadow may not really have been a master humorist, but then nobody is perfect.*

Some ladies in radio mysteries played a more dominant role than Margo Lane. Pam North of *Mr. and Mrs. North* was actually the chief detective of the team originated in the mystery novels by Frances and Richard Lockridge. Pam and Jerry North had their own radio series, and also appeared as guest stars—alternating with Nick Carter, Charlie Chan, Nero Wolfe, and even Superman—as the "Guest Detective" on the comedy-mystery-quiz, *Quick as a Flash,* hosted by Bill Cullen.

The contestants listened to several sketches, and finally a mystery, which they were to interrupt "Quick as a Flash" with an electronic signal as soon as they spotted the vital clue.

In one sketch, the Norths planned a vacation on an old houseboat. But naturally there was no vacation from murder for them.

PAM: Yoo hoo! Yoo hoo! May we come in?

RICKEY: Certainly . . .

JERRY: We're the couple who rented the houseboat. You Mr. Barton?

RICKEY: No, I'm not. He must be in one of the other rooms.

PAM: Oh, Jerry—this is cute!

JERRY: Depends on your point of view, Pam . . . Look . . . on the floor by the washstand . . .

* The Shadow was portrayed by a long line of actors, including Orson Welles. Bret Morrison played the part from 1944 to 1968, when he recorded two new dramas of *The Shadow* on MGM records with his original Margo, Grace Mathews.

RICKEY: Holy smoke, I hadn't seem 'im. The old geezer must have
     fainted . . .

JERRY: He was drowned.

RICKEY: Drowned? How can you tell?

PAM: You better take his word for it, Rickey. The contestants
     want to get to the murder clues . . .

Before the advent of the device in *avant garde* films,
radio actors were able to step outside the play for a moment,
and then back into it without destroying the scene.

Alice Frost played Pam (opposite Joseph Curtin as
Jerry), and she managed to sound a good deal like Gracie
Allen. She was a smart cookie who only sounded dumb. Most
men could easily accept that situation.

Pam and Jerry quickly spotted Rickey as the killer when
he told an *impossible* story of seeing old man Barton siphon
water *uphill* from the lake into his sink where he was
drowned.

JERRY: No one ever heard of water going up.

PAM: I have.

JERRY: When?

PAM: On Aunt Agatha. She got her feet wet in a rain storm and
     now she has water on the knee.

There were many twosomes in the mystery field, generally
composed of the familiar Holmes-Watson combination of the
keen detective and the dull-witted sidekick. There was Mr.
Keen, the kindly old tracer of lost persons, and Mike Clancy;
Ellery Queen and the loyal but bumbling Sergeant Velie;
Nick Carter, Master Detective, and his young newspaper
reporter friend, Scubby; and of course, Dick Tracy and Pat
Patton.

Sam Spade had his secretary, Effie, who sometimes appeared dense. and at other times womanly wise. Spade, himself, was his own comedian.

Some heroes, such as The Saint, were given to making witty observations, but Sam Spade could kid around with great style right in the middle of a murder investigation. Howard Duff, who played Spade, was a fine light comedian, and Lureen Tuttle as Effie was incomparable.

Dashiell Hammett's original Spade was a bit grim and at best sardonic, but in scripts and production under the supervision of William Spere, Spade developed a much lighter view of life.

"The Bow Window Caper" began as did all of Spade's cases with the detective calling in to his office.

EFFIE: Sam Spade Detective Agency.
SPADE: Hello, Sweetheart—it's only me.
EFFIE: Sam—why so modest?
SPADE: Women, Effie. "Age cannot wither nor custom stale their infinite variety . . . Against their incalculable wiles, mere man is a leaf in the wind . . ."
EFFIE: Sam—do you mean—? Who was she and how windy was it?
SPADE: Cyclonic, Effie!

As the story unfolded, it was difficult to pin down just which woman in the cast he was describing as practicing her "incalculable wiles." There was a seemingly mad wife of a doctor who was driving the office nurse dopey, not to mention what she was doing to her medic husband. Sam told the nurse he hoped he would not have as much trouble on the case as she had.

NURSE: Esther isn't jealous of your type . . .
SPADE: I feel heartened that you noticed I was different.
NURSE: Oh, I did, Mr. Spade. I really did.

SPADE: You don't seem particularly—umm—*nursey* to me either.
NURSE: I'm not— My, you have a fast pulse, Mr. Spade.
SPADE: Yes, I've been feeling weak the last few minutes . . .
NURSE: You don't eat enough apples, Mr. Spade . . .
SPADE (*narrating*): She left me with my mouth open, and no
  thermometer in it . . .

In the due course of time—thirty minutes, of course—
Spade discovered that it was all the familiar story of the
doctor trying to make his wife appear insane. If the ending
was no surprise, the audience really did not care. We had
too much fun getting there.

Like all radio writing, mystery scripts relied heavily on
the many uses of language, including plays-on-words, puns,
and devastating metaphors. At times the witticisms of radio
private eyes went over like a parakeet in a bulletproof
jacket. But when the airwaves were right, mystery humor
succeeded in tickling our funny bone with a freshly chilled
ice pick.

The entity that probably succeeded best in chilling us with
humor was Raymond, "Your Host" on *Inner Sanctum Mysteries.* There were many hosts to dramatic anthologies on
radio, from Cecil B. De Mille on *Lux Radio Theatre* to Mr.
First Nighter on *The First Nighter.* Quite a few were considerably spookier than Mr. De Mille. The old Hermit of
The Hermit's Cave gave out with a lot of cackling laughter
as he brooded over his rats and skulls. Generally, he was the
only one laughing.

The host of *Inner Sanctum* (originally portrayed by Raymond Edward Johnson, hence the origin of the first name)
did say something genuinely funny at times, under the supervision of producer Hyman Brown. "Good evening, friends
of the Squeaking Door . . . Spooking of baseball . . . no-

body's better equipped for double-headers then we are . . .
It's quite a sight . . . our team with nine players, and
eighteen heads . . . And 'Kill the Umpire?' In our league,
that's no idle threat . . ."

The humor may seem a bit dated, but it is to the past
that radio mysteries with all their gore and glee belong.
Remembering them still elicits an appreciative shiver. There
was good humor even in the mocking, challenging laugh of
The Shadow, and all his brethren.

9.

No Funny Answers, Please

"I have a lady in the balcony, Doctor!" Ed Rymers called out.

"Good," Dr. I.Q. said agreeably. "Now from the stage of the Bijou Theatre in Cleveland, Ohio, where *Gone With the Wind* is playing all this week, let me ask the young lady to repeat our famous Monument to Memory: the Thought-Twister. For ten silver dollars, repeat after me:

"'Jim is slim,' said Tim to Kim,

"'Jim is slim, Tim' to him said Kim."

"Uh . . . uh . . . ummm," said the young lady in the balcony. "'Bim is dim,' said Kim to . . . uh . . ."

"Oh, no," said Dr. I.Q. "I think you will find that is "'Pat is fat, said the cat to the rat; Fat is Pat, said Slat to Matt!' *But* a box of Snickers to that lady and two tickets to next week's production!"

Or at least that's the way it sounded to me back in the

forties. *Dr. I.Q.* was created by Lee Segal and played by
various announcers, including Lew Valentine, Jimmy Mc-
Clain, and Stan Vainrib. In spite of, or perhaps because of,
the Mental Banker being totally devoid of a sense of humor,
more jokes were made *about* him than any other quiz show
on the air. (Henry Morgan: "I have a lady in the balcony,
doctor/Oh, well, I'm sorry to have disturbed you."). One
suspects Dr. I.Q. is still up in a remote balcony, explaining
carefully to some lady, "No, it's Jim *is* slim, to him said
Tim . . ."

Somewhere along the way someone came up with the idea
for a quiz show that actually contained *entertainment*. One
of the best of these that offered music and comedy in addition to quiz questions was *Kay Kyser's Kollege of Musical
Knowledge*.

The comedy came from babbling idiot Ish Kabibble
(played by Mervyn Bogue) and froggy voiced Fergy. The
songs were by handsome Harry Babbitt and Georgia Carroll, Kyser's wife. The questions were answered by the audience, sometimes collectively, sometimes individually. It went
like this:

KYSER: Evenin' folks. How ya all? Tonight the old college is
    alive with jive, fizzing with quizzing; we're holding class
    at—students!
AUDIENCE: *Camp Anza!*
KYSER: Camp Anza, that's right, chillen—the Army calls it a "way
    station"—you wish for a way to get away, but before you find a
    way you're on your way . . .

Kyser's accent came from his residence in North Carolina,
although he had been born in Olatha, Kansas (in 1906).
Even though he became a "kollege" professor later, he was

once a college drop-out from the University of North Carolina when he found out leading a band paid more than even most established lawyers could hope to earn. The minor gimmick he developed for his dance band remote broadcasts grew to dominate the whole show. The *Kollege of Musical Knowledge* played chiefly to servicemen during World War II.

KYSER: Sergeant, is this right or wrong—"Fantasia" is not the name of a country.

SERGEANT: That's . . . ah . . . right.

KYSER: That's right, you're *r-r-right* . . . Benjamin Franklin founded the *Saturday Evening Post*—right or wrong?

SERGEANT: Right.

KYSER: He says . . . (*cackling laugh*) . . . he says—you're right! The *Post* is a fine magazine too.

FERGY: I like *Esquire* better.

KYSER: Oh, Fergy, you like *Esquire* better than the *Post*. When did you ever read *Esquire?*

FERGY: Oh, is there *reading* in it too?

The Ol' Professor received a bit of competition from another bandleader, Sammy Kaye, who began a contest involving baton waving called *So You Want to Lead a Band?* Horace Heidt played a latter-day Major Bowes by running a talent hunt for amateurs and young professionals. But neither of these orchestra front men could match Kay Kyser's success with an audience participation show.

Phil Baker did not lead a band but he played the accordion and told jokes. After considerable success as an early thirties radio comedian, Baker was introduced as the host of *Take It or Leave It*. The show began a series of questions with the one dollar question ("What President's picture appears one the one dollar bill?") and kept doubling the money all the way up to the gigantic grand prize, the sixty-four dollar question ("What is the name of Thomas Jefferson's home which appears on the five-cent piece?"). After the term became folk idiom for a tough problem, the show became titled *The Sixty-Four Dollar Question* and later hosts included Garry Moore and Eddie Cantor.

There were plenty of other quiz shows and audience participation shows that depended on joking masters of ceremonies—Art Linkletter's *House Party*, Jack Bailey's *Queen for a Day*, Walter O'Keefe's *Double or Nothing*, and Bob Hawk's *Bob Hawk Show*.

On a local radio level, Jack Eigen virtually invented the talk show, quizzing people for entertainment instead of rote answers for prizes. Eigen began his show in New York, moved it to St. Louis, and has settled at WMAQ Chicago where he continues it today. Barry Gray and Long John Nebel took over the New York audiences. Before his success on the television comedy *Hogan's Heroes*, Bob Crane conducted the best radio interview program on the West Coast from KNX Los Angeles.

For those network shows which despaired of finding a master of ceremonies as entertaining as a Jack Eigen, they simply tried bribing their listeners to tune in by offering them huge amounts of money via telephone calls. These were programs such as *Pot O' Gold* and *Stop the Music*.

Two programs more than any others relied on *comedy* mixed with their quiz questions. One dealt in clever verbal humor (*You Bet Your Life*), and the other with slapstick stunts (*Truth or Consequences*) which proved to be admirably suited to television in later years.

Truth or Consequences asked contestants questions that were generally impossible to answer since they were new versions of old gags. (Q. Why didn't the chicken cross the road a second time? *A.* Because he didn't want to be a double-crosser.) Then, if they missed, they had to pay the consequences, which might require a gentleman to spar a few rounds with Jack Dempsey, or a lady to give an elephant a bath.

The title goes back to an ancient parlor game. When radio announcer Ralph Edwards was required to scramble himself like an egg at a party in 1939 he got the idea for doing that sort of thing on the radio. Although he set out in life to be an English teacher, the radio business seemed to hound him all his life. When he was a high school junior in Oakland, California, Edwards wrote a script for a school broadcast, and acted the leading role. The radio station manager hired him to do regular scripts at the going rate of one dollar for each. At the University of California, Edwards went to school with radio performers Michael Rafetto and Barton Yarborough, cast members of *One Man's Family*. It was not until 1938 when he was destitute in New York that he got his first job as a radio announcer. Soon he was announcing *Against the Storm* and other soap operas—up to forty-five shows a week. *Truth or Consequences* became the forty-sixth and the most successful.

In a typical show, Edwards asked one particular lady contestant, "Why is life insurance like car polish? Now what's your—oh-oh, there's Beulah the buzzer. You didn't tell the truth so you must pay the consequences. Why is life insurance like car polish? It protects your finish."

Edwards proceeded to ask the young lady if she thought she could be as good a comedian as Fred Allen or Jack Benny if she had material as good as theirs to read. She had her doubts but nonetheless was hustled off stage to rehearse her comedy script. "Is she gone—she can't hear? Oh, what's going to happen to her . . ." Or rather to her husband. He was positioned behind a screen where she would not be able to see him. Every time she delivered a comedy line, he was going to be hit in the face with a lemon-meringue pie—a sure laugh-getter, as Edwards knew from years of experience. Finally the wife was brought back to the microphone to read her script. "Don't anybody give the gag away," Edwards urged the studio audience. *"Aren't we devils?"*

CONTESTANT: Hello, Ralphie boy.
EDWARDS: Hello, girl. I understand you just got married.
CONTESTANT: Yes, I married an X-ray technician—he was the only one who could see anything in me.

The audience's roar of laughter was all we could hear at home, but we could imagine that gooey mess hitting the husband in the face.

EDWARDS: Listen to them . . . see—it's the *delivery* that counts. Where did you meet your husband?
CONTESTANT: In a revolving door—and we've been going around together ever since.

Smack went another unseen pie into the woman's husband's face. Finally came the moment of further chagrin when the contestant was shown what she had been doing inadvertently to her husband.

The humor may have been primitive, but it was a lot gentler than today's jollies when the audience laughs at a dead man taking a funny pratfall after having his guts shot out by James Bond or Matt Helm.

The fun still goes on, on *Truth or Consequences,* now a syndicated TV show, although Ralph Edwards has retired to a position of executive producer while a young man named Bob Barker M.C.'s the festivities.

Humor more verbal and clever was exercised by Groucho Marx on *You Bet Your Life*. Some of the interviews with contestants were set up in advance and Groucho had a staff of writers, but a lot of his wit was genuinely ad lib. Although the audience participation show did not begin until 1947, Groucho had plenty of experience in radio. In the early thirties, he appeared with at least one other of the famous Marx Brothers—Chico—in routines similar to their madcap movies like *A Night at the Opera*. (Harpo, who never spoke in films, did do *occasional* radio appearances, where he whistled or honked horns.) Groucho was also a popular guest on such radio panel shows as *Information Please*. Humor on this show leaned in the direction of puns. John Kieran replied to the question as to the identity of Reza Pahlavi by saying "Reza Pahlavi is the ruler of Persia." Master of ceremonies Clifton Fadiman queried "Are you shah?" Kieran nodded. "Sultanly." Groucho must have felt there was room for him in radio.

When announcer George Fenneman ushered contestants before Groucho, he always informed them that if they said the "Secret Word" they would receive a cash bonus. The word was usually something like "turkey" and others that don't come up in conversations, even with Groucho, every day. Then it may not have been a case of *You Bet Your Life,* but you risked some deep cuts in your ego by the time Groucho got through with you.

One contestant was only a high school boy.

GROUCHO: How old are you?
CONTESTANT: Sixteen.
GROUCHO: Are you married?

CONTESTANT: N-no . . .

GROUCHO: Where do you take your school siestas?

CONTESTANT: Hollywood High . . .

GROUCHO: What do you want to do when you get out of school?

CONTESTANT: I want to be a comedian—

GROUCHO: There's always room for another comedian—but not on the same program as *me* . . . To be a comedian, you have to have some jokes.

CONTESTANT: I have jokes . . . What category would you like?

GROUCHO: Boy, am I glad I got that annuity . . . You pick your own category.

CONTESTANT: I'll tell you the one about the time I went hunting. I once shot an elephant in my pajamas. How he got into them I'll never know.

GROUCHO: That's a good joke—is it one of your own?

CONTESTANT: No. It's one of yours.

Then came the quiz questions. If the contestant struck out, Groucho would bark: "Okay, for fifty bucks—who is buried in Grant's Tomb?" At least one contestant gave the wrong answer.

So it went. Joe Kelly quizzed *Quiz Kids;* Jack Barry questioned both the young on *Juvenile Jury* and the old on *Life Begins at Eighty;* and telephone quiz-masters like Bert Parks put questions to the whole country.

Where did they all go? Some of them went to daytime television. But in these days of trips around the world for prizes, who would care about Dr. I.Q.'s ten silver dollars? On the route to all that loot, who could take the meddlesome interruptions of one of the world's great comedians like Groucho Marx? There's a question for you.

10.

Thanks for the Memories

HOPE: How do you do, Ladies and Gentlemen.

This is Bob "Camp Roberts" Hope telling you to put Pepsodent on your brush and use plenty of traction and none of your teeth will be missing in action . . . I had a nice trip up here . . . you know these lightning Greyhounds? Well, this was a shuffling Peekenense . . . The driver was very careful every time he passed through a town—he slowed down to fifty and put aside the magazine he was reading . . . And if it was a really big town he'd make the blonde get off his lap . . . I asked the driver how fast we were going—he said "I don't know—the speedometer never works unless the wheels are touching the ground . . ."

In the era of radio, Bob Hope talked even faster than he does in television today. The lines were fired in machine-gun rapidity, appropriately enough for soldier audiences sometimes only yards away from real machine-gun chatter. "This is Bob 'Coast Guard' Hope . . ." "This is Bob 'Camp Pendleton Marine Base' Hope . . ." "This is Bob 'Use Pepsodent 'Cause Your Girl Won't Let You Squeeze 'Er, if You Got Vacancies under Your Breezer' Hope . . ." Out shot one-line gags one after another, a joke every three seconds. The audience did not have time to stop laughing. And what laughter! Never was there an audience more desperately in need of the escape of laughter, and never did they reward a comedian with more yowls, screams, whistles, and applause. The bedlam of appreciation never actually stopped during a wartime Bob Hope monologue. It only tapered off long enough for Hope to yell another one-liner that set off the whole torrent of uproar again. Wave after wave of laughter beat in on a listening America.

Hope is a wise-cracker, whatever his subject. He could make cracks about his own scoop-nose being the inspiration for the V-2 rocket launcher. He could say that they had made President Roosevelt's dog, Falla, a second lieutenant in the Army, but the dog had not been happy—he was older than all the other second lieutenants just out of West Point. His speed and delivery were the same. He was always fast, witty, and slightly stinging. He could be irreverent without really offending anyone, perhaps because he was as insulting to his own appearance—his ski nose, his receding hair, his inflated hips—as he was to the senators and generals who lead the country. During the wartime pressure for patriotism and service to country, he offered the escape valve of not taking everything *that* seriously.

Jerry Colonna's total irreverence to logic itself played well against Hope's wry attitude toward institutions. After Hope's monologue and the first breezy song from Frances Langford ("Don't Sit Under the Apple Tree with Anyone Else But Me" one chance out of three), the telephone would ring and Hope would blithely pick it up.

COLONNA: Hope hello. Colonna is this.
HOPE: Colonna, why are you talking backwards?
COLONNA: Put the nickel in upside down.
HOPE: That wouldn't have anything to do with it, Colonna.
COLONNA: Okay.
      (*Sound: Animal bellowing and snorting.*)
HOPE: What's that, Colonna?
COLONNA: I'm pulling the buffalo out by his tail.
HOPE: That's impossible.
COLONNA: I don't ask questions. I just have fun!

That slogan certainly reflected the radio character of Jerry Colonna. He could show up anytime during the show claiming to be a college professor, building contractor, United States Senator, a sword swallower. His attitude was that not only is history bunk, but the roles we play in society are bunk. Everybody was a phony, only posing as what he pretended to be. Colonna could pose just as well as any of them.

While he deviated from icon worship, Colonna's disrespect for reality was never carried to the point of total insanity. Before he could get too far out, he was always brought down to earth. He ran into typical trouble during a two-way radio conversation with Hope from a P-38 that had been shot up by Japanese Zeroes.

COLONNA: I'll be okay, Hope. I'll just eat out of this box labeled "Bird seed" and I'll be able to fly away on my own.
HOPE: Colonna, that's impossible.
COLONNA (*gulps*):   Okay, Hope, I've eaten it. Here I go out of the plane.
      (*Whistling dive; thunderous crash.*)
HOPE: What happened?

COLONNA: Wrong box, Hope.

HOPE: What?

COLONNA: "Bird *shot*"—not "bird *seed*."

Colonna's spot on the show fit in well with the general aura Bob Hope projected. Which gave the listener two choices simultaneously: the opportunity to laugh *with* him when he was demolishing one of a hundred targets; and the choice to laugh *at* him when he, himself, played the self-inflated bore. Thus his one-liners might hit hard, but somehow they never offended. And when one of his gag lines inflated his own ego, there was always somebody around to stick a sharp retort into the balloon. It might be Colonna or one of his several announcers like Bill Goodwin, or more than likely, that man-crazy old maid, Vera Vague (portrayed by Barbara Jo Allen.) Her name was misnomer, since she was far from Vague but clear-witted and razor-edged in her humor.

When Hope explained to Vera that the Marines in their audience always attacked an enemy from all sides, "squeezing and squeezing," she stuck out her tongue at them in a hostile manner. Hope told her to stop it.

VERA: It seemed like a good idea at the time!

HOPE: I suppose at one time *you* seemed like a good idea.

VERA: You say such clever things, Mr. Hope. Really, I wish I had your head. It'd look so nice stuffed over the mantelpiece. . . . These Marines are so wonderful. I wish my boy friend Waldo had joined up with them.

HOPE: What branch is Waldo in now?

VERA: Usually the one overlooking Hedy Lamarr's window!

Unlike most of the successful radio comedians, Hope never developed a large supporting cast of regulars. Colonna and Vera Vague were the only ones to last any length of time.

Sly old Jack Kirkwood appeared once as a Salvation Army Santa Claus and kept coming back on a number of later shows with his running gag of "Put something in the pot, boy." But Hope mostly worked with his announcers, girl vocalists, and his bandleaders, like Skinnay Ennis.

Ennis gave rise to innumerable "skinny" jokes. He was so skinny that

1. he used himself as a pipe cleaner on his own pipes.
2. when he let the water out of the tub, he was washed out to Santa Monica.
3. when he fought a duel with Frank Sinatra, neither could see the other standing sideways.

Hope seemed to know a lot more answers than we did, but happily he always got put down harder than we ever did in real life. After all, Lana Turner never actually *laughed* at our love-making, as she did Hope's. Admiral Nimitz never suggested to us that we should join the *Japanese* Navy—for the good of the United States. Those were put-downs of an Olympian nature.

One such guest star who tweeked the ski nose was Ida Lupino.

HOPE: Well, Ida, you look sweet as apple cida'. Yes, sir.
IDA: He weaves a beautiful web, doesn't he?
HOPE: You're a small girl, Ida. You hardly come up to my chin.
IDA: Which one?
HOPE: Those aren't chins—that's a staircase for my Adam's apple . . .

Bob Hope's backyard-type personality, his gift of conversation, made him the kind of man the radio listener wouldn't mind having over to play cards with and talk about Roosevelt running for a third term. Hope seemed pretty much like the rest of us, but, *at the same time*, with our gift of gab magnified to the thousandth power. Who did not daydream of being at a party and being miraculously gifted with the power to evoke appreciative laughter with every remark? "This drink is so strong, they are going to use my head as a replacement for the Telstar satellite . . . Those drapes are so loud they are going to wake up Spiro Agnew . . . Miss Jones's dress is cut so low that . . ." Only it never works for us. Only Bob Hope.

Hope seemed to earn some of the liberties granted a serviceman in wartime, given him as a sort of honorary serviceman himself. He managed to get away with saying things on the air denied to most civilians at that time. While Hope's humor was not really objectionable, and even seems mild today, it was spicy for the era of radio comedy.

In one sketch before the troops, Hope courted a girl in a park, a bit more bashfully than usual.

HOPE: Some park.
GIRL: Some park.
HOPE: Some grass.
GIRL: Some grass.
HOPE: Some dew.
GIRL: *I don't.*

The PTA groups over the country forgave Bob Hope like the prodigal son. They were caught up by his brash charm like the rest of us.

You had to feel a bit sorry for him, though, when Bing Crosby belittled his golf game and the knock-knees in his knickers. But Hope had brought it all on himself by talking about Bing's hair getting as thin as a cheese sandwich at Jack Benny's house, and by referring to Bing's race horses running right past the finish line and into the glue factory.

The 1940s were full of classic feuds—Jack Benny vs. Fred Allen, Joe Louis vs. Max Schmeling, the Human Torch vs. the Sub-Mariner, Churchill vs. Hitler—but of all these epic conflicts, none was carried on with a higher verve and vitality than the one between the ski-nosed comic and the old groaner.

On one broadcast, Hope had just finished insulting Crosby's loud jackets, his ancient worn-out race horses, and his growing family of sons, when Bing arrived.

CROSBY: Sorry I'm late, Bob. I had trouble finding a place to park.

HOPE: What do you mean? The stable's right outside.

CROSBY: Is that what that was? I thought it was your dressing room. It was—last time I was on your show.

HOPE: That was last time. They moved me out to the garage. It was the least they could do.

CROSBY: How do you mean that?

HOPE: I asked for a raise.

CROSBY: That takes nerve. You haven't been able to get a raise out of your audience in years.

HOPE: Tell me, Bing, with so much hot air and those ears why don't you take off?

CROSBY: The down-draft from your nose prevents it.

HOPE: Bing, why do we fight? You know, I really like you.

CROSBY: Only when you've been out on those Army bases too long.

Unlike most of the other classic feuds, the one between Hope and Crosby outlasted the forties, and continued into the fifties and sixties. In commenting on one of the more recent "Road" pictures, *Road to Utopia*, Crosby said: "This is one of the cleanest of the 'Road' pictures, because a certain fat portion of Hope's anatomy was dragging along most of the way, wiping up the road."

However, Hope had the ultimate insult for Crosby in the *Utopia* picture. For the first time, Hope took the girl away from crooner-lover Crosby.

The Road to Rio was the first *Road* picture with Crosby and the saronged Dorothy Lamour. It was one of Hope's first film successes following *The Big Broadcast of 1938* in which he introduced his theme song-to-be, "Thanks for the Memory."

Bob Hope always closed each radio show with a serious narration in which he recalled all the wonderful memories he had of being able to entertain all the men at that base or hospital. If he cared to, he could go into a long list of memories from his own eventful life.

Born May 26, 1904, in Eltham, England, as Leslie Townes Hope, he was shortly known as "Bob" Hope in Cleveland, Ohio, U.S.A. The years went by. He was a delivery boy for his brother's butcher shop . . . a dancing instructor . . . a saxophone player . . . a Golden Gloves boxer . . . a blackface minstrel . . . a Broadway star in *Ballyhoo of 1932* and *Roberta* . . . and finally a star in movies and on radio.

Bob Hope has not competely deserted radio, even in the era of television. He has a series of five-minute monologue programs syndicated to many U.S. stations, and his old half-hour shows are continually being re-broadcast on the Armed Forces Radio in Europe and throughout the world. Appropriately enough the shows done for servicemen over twenty years ago are still entertaining servicemen—the sons of the first group.

Of course, Hope reigns over a vast empire of which radio is only a small fraction. Besides his interests in a horde of

corporations valued by *Time* magazine as being worth between 150 and 500 million dollars, he continues to do television shows, a few records and a continuing stream of feature films for theaters in which, although well into his sixties,
he continues to portray at least ostensibly middle-aged heroes
with considerable believability.

Time has touched Bob Hope lightly. His appeal to audiences is much the same as it has been for more than thirty
years. Many young people like him, despite his attacks on
hippies in his comedy and his attacks on peace protestors in
more serious moments. Hope remains a symbol of the man
who is "in the know," who isn't fooled by sham. As such, he
will always remain a hero to those who can also see through
the pompous asses of the world but who lack his wit to so
puncture them with a burst of machine-gun-like spurts of
laughter.

Bob Hope is one of the great irreplacable stars who will
never outwear their welcome.

11.

Songs and Laughter

"Next week the Kraft Music Hall stage is again gwine to resound with fun and frolic, music and madness, song and story and possibly a potpourri. As honored guest . . . Mischa Levitzky, the renowned pianist; Joe Venuti, hot fiddler extraordinary; the Parks Sisters and the Radio Rogues . . . Bob Burns . . . and your humble servant, Moe Crosby."

That's how Bing Crosby would typically sign off his long-running Kraft Music Hall show—in the verbal potpie style that was his trademark on radio. It came out as a series of radar-like blips . . . a rolling, hill-and-dale cadence in which he managed to sound when speaking as he did when crooning, "Ba-ba-ba-boo, baba-ba-boo, ba-ba-ba-boo-boo."

Crosby first gained fame as a romantic singer, but he was

too easygoing, too good natured and likable ever to be completely believable in that role. Besides, part of his charm was that he never took anything *too* seriously, including himself. He made light of his lover image and all his other little traits, and emerged as a fine light comedian, one who would be at home at the best country clubs in the nation. Only Bob Hope was capable of making Bing Crosby look like a straight man.

Whether doing comedy skits, romantic scenes, or singing, it was Bing Crosby of all the idols of the thirties who did everything he attempted almost equally well. He could sing "Temptation" with soul-stirring hunger, but when handed a script of patter—the light, easygoing lines of humor between songs—he did not merely walk through it like most singers, but tried to get laughs out of often tired and obligatory gags. Of course, most importantly, he never *seemed* to be trying hard.

Bing's thing was casualness. He either forgot or pretended to forget the words of songs and whistled or on occasion hummed with his mouth open. Hope called him "the groaner," and one critic described his vocal style as a "lad with his voice changing, singing into a rain barrel." Another spoke of his comedy style as combining "the dead pan school of slapstick comic and . . . the insouciant ogle of the professional masher . . ." The effect was that Bing was at home anywhere, sure of himself in the uncertain time of the Depression. His polysyllabic rush of words—a combination of Bing's ad-libbing and the scripts of his longtime producer and writer, Bill Morrow—seemed to mark him a professional man just out of college; at the same time, he moved with the speed and confidence of a poolroom shark.

Bing was born Harry Lillis Crosby in 1904 in Tacoma, Washington, one of the seven children of Kate and Harry Lowe Crosby. (Two brothers, Everett and Larry, assisted Bing in his business matters, and of course, Bob became a band-leader and popular singer in his own right.) His nickname came from a comic strip he was mad for as a boy, called *The Bingville Bugle.* He seemed headed for a law career, trying to earn his degree at Gonzaga University, but he spent so much time with a student orchestra that he had to drop out in his second year. For a time he was one of the three Rhythm Boys with Paul Whiteman's band, but soon he was doing a single.

Crosby made some short comedies for Mack Sennett, sang some songs in *The Big Broadcast of 1932* film, and had week-day radio shows on first CBS and then NBC. In 1936, he became singing host of the *Kraft Music Hall* on NBC and his fame became secure.

After that, thanks to brother Everett's management, Bing seemed to take off in all directions. He was on the radio, on records, in movies; in time, he owned a gold mine, an employment agency, a music publishing company, two boxers and one girl's baseball team. But most noteworthy of all, Bing owned a string of race horses. Those slow-running nags accounted for as many jokes as Jack Benny's parsimony, Bob Hope's ski nose, and the bags under Fred Allen's eyes.

CROSBY: I'm thinking about entering one of my horses in the Kentucky Derby.

ANNOUNCER KEN CARPENTER: I'm thinking about going a few rounds with Joe Louis.

CROSBY: Do I detect a note of the caustic? I breed some of the finest horseflesh in the country.

CARPENTER: I know. A butcher in Encino recommended it to me.

The all-purpose gag was one accusing Crosby of wearing one of his horse's blankets for a sports jacket.

On the *Kraft Music Hall*, Bing gagged it up with co-stars from his films like W. C. Fields who made *Mississippi* with him; Dorothy Lamour, his saronged romantic interest from the *Road* pictures; and, of course, Bob Hope.

HOPE: It's good to appear on *your* show for a change, Bing.
CROSBY: Yes, *we* pay.
HOPE: Pepsodent toothpaste is just as tasty as Kraft cheese.
CROSBY: Now I understand about those sandwiches you serve at rehearsal on your show.

Crosby also proved his versatility by discussing serious music with Leopold Stokowski and José Iturbi, sang love songs with Peggy Lee and Irish songs with Pat O'Brien. Between songs he would banter with announcer Ken Carpenter and bandleader, John Scott Trotter. The stout orchestra leader was the victim of almost as many "fat" jokes as Jack Benny's announcer, Don Wilson.

For the first year of the *Kraft* show, Bing also had Wilson for his announcer, and his first orchestra leader was Jimmy Dorsey. After the band finished their number, it became traditional for the star of a variety show to chat briefly with the leader. Since no one could see him wave the baton, this bit of dialogue would be all the personal "exposure" he would get. Some orchestra leaders, such as Frank DeVol on the *Jack Smith-Dinah Shore Show* became excellent comedians in their own right. Jimmy Dorsey only proved adequate for a few harmless exchanges.

CROSBY: Jimmy, I want to tell you that was a very stylish piece of clarineting.
DORSEY: It should be. I stayed up all night practicing.
CROSBY: Why don't you work daytimes, like other people?
DORSEY: Then when would I play golf?

CROSBY: Play golf! Do you mean to stand here in front of me and tell me you allow a mere pastime to interfere with your professional career? My boy, in that direction lies madness. And another thing . . . see that you don't keep me waiting on the first tee tomorrow.

Bing traded quips with many people on the K.M.H. but with no one more often or more memorably than with the Arkansas Traveler, Bob Burns (who played a gigantic moose call of his own invention, the bazooka, which gave its name to the World War II weapon).

CROSBY: Now, Bob, as I understand it, your home town, Van Buren, Arkansas, gave you quite a homecoming the other day. Tell me, boy, how does it feel to be met at the train with three bands?

BURNS: . . . I have touched the high spot in my life . . . Besides the Van Buren band there was the band from Fort Smith and the Jug band from Babylon, another suburb of Van Buren. I never saw such a parade in my life. They had ox teams, men leading hound dogs—and some more men leading some of my kinfolks that they had brought in from the mountains . . . I think one of the main reasons why they gave me the homecoming was so they could have an excuse for bringing my relatives into town. Van Buren wanted something to laugh at. I left Van Buren in the first place because they laughed at me. They laughed at me this time till I started telling them jokes. Then they stopped . . . Mama told me how it affected Papa when he heard me play the bazooka over the radio . . . When I was half way through my solo, Papa got up and walked over and took the radio in his arms—and threw it out the window . . .

Bing Crosby continued to do radio until 1962 when he concluded a daily series with Rosemary Clooney. His TV shows today seem much like visualizations of his old *Music Hall* shows. Bing *has* grown older, but not quite like the rest of us—he seems to add years at about the same lackadaisical speed as one of his old race horses.

THE JAZZ SINGER

Al Jolson has a continuing reputation as "the world's greatest entertainer," a reputation that has even survived him. There are many reasons: his forty years of success on the stage; his starring in the first successful talking motion picture, *The Jazz Singer*, in 1927; two hit movies based on his life with Larry Parks lip-synching Jolson's singing voice; the songs from those movies of the forties that still sell today on Decca records; and to Jolson's triumphant return to radio.

After the release of the enormously successful *Jolson Story* movie, Al Jolson became feverishly sought by all the big variety shows of radio. His first big comeback was with Bing Crosby, whose relaxed style played well against Jolson's constant animation. Soon, he was doing several guest appearances each week—he hit a record high of ten shows in one week. On the *Burns and Allen* program, Gracie Allen asked "Al, why don't you get your own show?" Jolie replied: "What? And only be on the radio once a week!"

Jolson was on the radio a long time. His bombastic, all-out delivery of limitless energy was actually not ideal for the sightless medium of radio, which interrupted his face-to-face love-affair with his audience, but somehow he did succeed in transmitting much of his tremendous personal magnetism across the air-waves.

From Lew Dockstader's Minstrels and lavish Shubert musicals, Jolson made his first radio appearance in 1929 on NBC's *Pure Oil Band* special. Jolson ad-libbed a somewhat cryptic comment on Clara Bow's sleeping habits that inspired a flood of protest letters.

NBC soon forgave him and launched him on his first weekly series of fifteen shows for Chevrolet, *Presenting Al Jolson* in 1932. After this successful trial run, Jolson became the original host of the *Kraft Music Hall* in 1933, for thirty-one shows with Paul Whiteman's Orchestra and Deems Taylor. Jolson not only sang and told jokes, but afforded his audience the mind-staggering pleasure of hearing his acting abilities in Shakespearean dramas and adaptations of classics like *The Man without a Country*. Deems Taylor must have been put upon to restrain his usual activity as critic.

For his next series, *Shell Chateau*, in 1935, Jolson left the dramatics to guests such as Leslie Howard and Bette Davis. He still got in on the comedy, though, insisting his writers give him a funny line for every gag given a guest comedian, such as the ubiquitous George Jessel, or newcomer Maxie Rosenbloom.

JOLSON: You know that guy, Joe Louis who knocked out Primo Carnera the other night? Well, you should have heard what I told him—I told him plenty. I told him he was nothing but a big palooka, a big sissy, I told him I'd blacken both his eyes, and bust his nose in, too.

ROSENBLOOM: You told Joe Louis all that! What did he say?

JOLSON: What could he say? I hung up on him.

ROSENBLOOM: I'll never forget the time in one of my fights my opponent was down and I begged him to get up.

JOLSON: You begged him to get up? Why?

ROSENBLOOM: He was on top of me.

Jolson switched his fictional locale from the *Shell Chateau* to *Cafe Trocadero* in 1936. In the forties, he appeared on his own *Colgate Toothpaste Show* (1942) and in various guest appearances on such programs as the *Lux Radio Theatre*. In 1947, after his triumphant come-back due to the biographical movie, he took over the chores on the program he had vacated years before, the *Kraft Music Hall*.

To assist him with the comedy passages, Jolson had pianist and humorist, Oscar Levant, whose wit was familiar from the genuinely intellectual quiz show, *Information Please*. A typical comment to Jolson from the acid Levant went: "The first thing I do when I get up in the morning is brush my teeth, and sharpen my tongue."

When Jolson moved the show temporarily to New York from its regular Hollywood base, he reminisced to Levant.

JOLSON: . . . I remember when I was a kid. I used to stand outside Luchow's Restaurant with my nose pressed against the window, and watch the celebrities eat. Just for old times' sake, I went down . . . and pressed my nose against that same window. A man came out and said, "Look bud . . . you've been standing out here for forty years. Come in and have a free meal."

LEVANT: You went in, of course.

JOLSON: Of course . . . Ah, those were great days, Oscar. I wish I had been born thirty years earlier.

LEVANT: You were . . . *I* went to a concert at Carnegie Hall.

JOLSON: How'd you like it?

LEVANT: Not so good. I wasn't playing that night.

Certain critics always detected Jolson's tongue planted firmly in cheek. In a voice permanently touched with a suggestion of minstrel-show dialect, Al Jolson would occasionally strike an apparently inappropriate comedic note. When he breaks up "Mammy" with "Doncha know me— its yoah leddle boay—" he seems to not be taking the pathos of the situation seriously and to have revealed himself with a vocal wink to be, perhaps more than anything else, a singing comedian.

"GOODNIGHT, MRS. CALABASH!"

The tradition of the singer telling jokes between songs spread through Radioland. Throughout the thirties and forties we heard Jack Owens and Johnny Desmond joking with Don McNeill on *The Breakfast Club*, Western balladeer Curley Bradley joshing with Ransome Sherman on *Club Matinee*, and even opera stars like Lily Pons and Lauritz Melchior trading jokes on variety shows. On the local level, New York City listened to chuckling Arthur "Red" Godfrey, the Warbling Banjoist, who eventually went network. All the Midwest listened to the good variety shows from the WBBM Air Theatre, Wrigley Building, Chicago with tenor Billy Leech swapping gags with host Jim Conway and grumpy commentator Paul Gibson, to singer and comic Patrick O'Reily, and to *The Goldcoast Show* which featured fully dramatized skits, comedian George Watson, and Johnny, George and Fritz of the King's Jesters singing trio, and ten million commercials. The South followed the *Grand Old Opry* from WSM Nashville with Roy Acuff and Minnie Pearl.

It would be difficult to exactly categorize certain old vaudevillians like Jimmy Durante, but his act depended heavily on his singing and piano playing. His greatest success on radio came when he was teamed with the rather serious comic Garry Moore, who liked to think of himself as radio's answer to straight-faced Buster Keaton. Seldom has there been a greater contrast between members of a comedy team.

In one sketch, Durante and Moore played college students.

MOORE: Jimmy, the final exams are coming up this week and we
really need some help. Gee, I wish the school had an advisory
board—someone we could ask questions of, like Lana Turner
or Betty Grable.

DURANTE: Lana Turner and Betty Grable? Wot kinda questions
could we ask dem?

MOORE: He's led such a sheltered life.

DURANTE: Well, I don't know. Ya know, Junior, dis year college
is a serious ting wid me. I get to the classroom every morning
at four o'clock.

MOORE: Four o'clock in the morning! What do you take?

DURANTE: Oh, the usual ting—a pail and a mop . . . First, last
and always I'm a gentleman of culture . . . (*Sings.*)
Now what I say may sound absurd, but believe me it's true,
I've seen every opera and I'll name dem for you:
"Tales of the Vienna Rolls," "Madam Buttermilk,"
"The Sextette from Leechee Nuts,"
And "The Quartet from Rigor Mortis" which I know from
memory,
I coach sopranos and tenors in dere parts,
Cause I'm Durante, the patron of da arts . . .

Jimmy sang all that while as invisible on radio as his friends
"Umbriago" and "Mrs. Calabash" (to whom he always said
good night, "wherever you are" at the end of every broadcast).

Durante had a long climb to the top. Only an incredibly
few short years after being born in 1893 on New York's
Lower East Side, Jimmy was thumping an upright piano in
an old nightclub on the Bowery—one so obscure that today
he can't even remember the name of the place. He did not
read music, but like so many of his skills he just somehow
picked it up, drowning out the sour notes with his own voice.

By 1927, Durante had become a full-time vaudeville per-

former with the team of Clayton, Jackson and Durante.
Movies beckoned, and for a time he was teamed with Buster
Keaton in a series of shorts. This contrast between the dead-
panning Keaton and the ebullient Durante was similar to the
contrast that was attempted between Jimmy and his radio
partner, Garry Moore.

Moore had tried a number of other careers—playwright,
news announcer, sports commentator—but then, after writing material for the show, he became a comedian on the
Club Matinee program out of Chicago. It was as a comic
that Moore had his greatest success—of the rather cool, self-
contained variety—one with seemingly little in common with
the frantic, unpretentious Durante. Yet the contrast between
them worked so well that when they appeared together on a
special variety hour, they immediately gained their own regular series.

MOORE: I've taken on a new job, Jimmy—
DURANTE: A new job, Junior?
MOORE: Yes, Jimmy, a new job in the shoddy, shabby and shady
    suburb in the Shropshire section of Massachusetts—with a
    flashy, trashy but fairly fashionable cash haberdashery . . .
    I've trying to earn enough money to take out our singing
    star, Suzanne Ellers.
DURANTE: Yeah, Junior—she's just the kind of *femme* to cherchez!

Although they have gone their separate ways, each retains
a substantial and faithful following. Durante's ingratiating il-
literacy was never played against a better foil than young,
earnest Garry Moore. While Moore's substantial abilities have
occasionally been underestimated, it is Durante of the two
who is the true genius—one of the monumental figures of show
business.

While Durante is difficult to neatly pigeonhole, Eddie Cantor can be described as a singer who became *primarily* known as a comedian.

Cantor climbed up through vaudeville, the *Ziegfeld Follies* and other Broadway hits like so many others, did almost from the first, his songs like "Makin' Whoopee" were touched with the comic (unlike those of his friend and contemporary, Al Jolson, which were mostly romance and nostalgia). All of his life, Eddie Cantor devoted an inordinate amount of his time and effort to benefits, charities, and other worthy causes. It might be said his motivation was the compulsive need to be loved that marks so many performers, but Cantor undeniably achieved a lot of good.

His first radio appearance was an experimental broadcast over a New Jersey station in 1921. Characteristically, he solicited funds for the Salvation Army on it.

Eddie Cantor's first regular series began in 1931 after an appearance on the Rudy Vallee show (which helped launch so many radio stars). He continued on radio for nearly thirty years, working for various sponsors such as Chase and Sanborn coffee and Ipana toothpaste, ending his radio career with a low-budgeted syndicated series featuring only himself and his announcer, Jimmy Wallington, doing skits between phonograph records.

During his prime period in the forties, Cantor gained fame and a few real votes by running for President of the United States as a gag—much as Pat Paulsen, Pogo, and Snoopy were to do at a later time. The four musical notes that went with the chant of "We-want-Can-tor!" became almost as well known as his regular theme of "One Hour with You" or his bulging "banjo" eyes.

Unlike many comedians of the era, Cantor never had a large cast of supporting regulars. He introduced many singers—such as Dinah Shore, Deanna Durbin, and Bobby Breen—who became great successes in their own right, but the only characters on a par with Senator Claghorn or Rochester or the Old Timer he ever developed, himself, were the language-scrambling Greek chef, Parkyakarkas (Harry Einstein), who later opened up a restaurant on a show of his own; and Bert Gordon, the "Mad Russian." Gordon played the typical "funny foreigner" of the time, the outlander with customs so strange that he was suspected of lunacy by good solid Americans.

On one of his shows during World War II, Eddie Cantor and another of his announcers, Harry Von Zell, were preparing to travel East by train when they met the Mad Russian at the depot.

RUSSIAN: *How do you do!*

CANTOR: Russian, what are you doing here?

RUSSIAN: I am a travel agent. In fact, traveling is mine hobo.

CANTOR: You don't mean *hobo*, you mean *hobby*.

RUSSIAN: You travel on your salary, I'll travel on mine!

CANTOR: Have you ever arranged a trip for anyone else?

RUSSIAN: Yes. I was on a train for eight days with Hedy Lamarr going to San Francisco.

VON ZELL: On a train with Hedy Lamarr eight days? You should have got there in one day.

RUSSIAN: Ah-hah. I was so disappointed!

While his cast of regulars may have been small, Cantor always managed to come up with great guest stars, like Jolson, John Barrymore, Crosby, W. C. Fields, Basil Rathbone, and

Cary Grant. A typical Cantor finish would be a comedy duet with a guest like Grant.

GRANT (*singing*):
    Since to war our silk has gone,
    Women paint their stockings on.
    You would think they're wearing nylons, but they ain't.
CANTOR (*singing*):
    Now I don't mean to be mean,
    But from some legs I have seen,
    I could swear there must be wrinkles in the paint!

As the laughter and applause died down, Eddie Cantor would segue into a sentimental version of "I Love to Spend One Hour with You." As the orchestra played the theme under, he would plead for one of his favorite charities; he would say something personal to Ida and his famous five daughters; he would sincerely invite you to sample his sponsor's product; and the music and Eddie Cantor would fade away on the summer air for another week. Although he always admitted to being overshadowed by his legendary contemporary, Al Jolson, it is interesting to note that Eddie Cantor's career never really had the ups and downs that Jolson's did. Eddie Cantor was always a man the American public was ready to welcome into their homes.

12.

The Thirty-nine-year-old Skinflint

"This is Jack Benny; now there will be a pause for everyone to say 'Who cares?'" Those were the first words Jack Benny ever said on radio, but certainly not the last. He found out that many millions of people cared. His fictional character grew much too vain, though, to have been so self-deprecating in later years. By the forties, he was answering the telephone on his radio show by saying, "Jell-O again—this is Jack Benny, star of stage, screen and radio; laundry done cheap."

Benny's vanity, stinginess, touchiness about his age all came about "accidentally," Jack reported in a recent broadcast interview. Those characteristics hardly represent Benny's off-mike personality, but they were the jokes that seemed to work best for him. (One can hardly grapple with the concept of Jack Benny as a compulsive girl-chaser or a drunk, but those roles were once tried by him with imperfect results.)

On closer examination, however, the radio character of Jack

Benny was not such an "accident." He was not an active comedy writer, like his fabled nemesis, Fred Allen, but he was a genius at comedy *editing*. Jack Benny could invariably select the joke that would work best for him. Moreover, he not only shaped his own comedy character, but helped mold the public personalities of the other members of his cast—one of the truly "all star" casts in entertainment history.

For instance, when Dennis Day first auditioned to be the boy singer on the Benny show, he was so nervous he really did respond to his name being called by saying "Yes, please." Benny responded, "That's *cute*—keep it." He had less influence in making Don Wilson a fat man or Phil Harris a heavy drinker and an appreciator of feminine beauty, but he saw how exploitable those jokes were for them. (Can you imagine making jokes about Orson Welles being fat, or about Tommy Dorsey drinking too much?)

According to the script, Jack Benny found Eddie "Rochester" Anderson on a train as a porter, and put him to work as a personal valet. In reality, Jack Benny hired Rochester, then a song and dance man, for a small part on the show, recognized his potential and made him a regular. Rochester was a marked innovation at the time—a Negro who, though he talked huskily, was virtually without a trace of Southern dialect; and one who frequently was smarter than his boss, as well.

Benny did an even better job of talent scouting when it came to Mary Livingstone. He found her working for the May Company department store in Los Angeles and made her his wife. It was not until a few years later that he discovered she could also be a talented comedienne, playing a brash and breezy girl friend. Like Jack himself, Mary has always had a good ear for the kind of material that worked best for Jack and for herself, being very, very hard to please. "She's a tough kid," Benny has said.

Jack Benny saw his radio character and all his cast as being prototypes of *real* people, not burlesque caricatures. Everybody knows a tightwad. "Benny is as tight as Uncle Ed," a listener would muse. "That Phil Harris is as girl-crazy as my brother-in-law," another would conclude. Fat people all over America used to glory in the jokes about Don Wilson. It proved there was somebody fatter in this world than they.

Benny felt that the audience could see itself through his show. "If someone pulls a gag on me about my having false teeth, ninety-eight per cent of the audience who have false teeth will laugh. The other two per cent would, too, but their gums are still sore," Benny observed.

Benny was one of the gentlest gentlemen in radio comedy, and one of the most successful. "*Frustration* can be funny, not pain." It can be funny if the young man is forever interrupted by father, servants, comrades, as he tries to make love to his girl. If he is forever frustrated by her lying stone dead it is no longer comic but tragic. "If it hurts, it isn't funny," Benny believed. The point might well have been debated by W. C. Fields, Chaplin, or even Fred Allen, but it is the credo upon which Benny has always based his career.

Jack Benny created himself of a lad born as Benny Kubelsky in Waukegan, Illinois, on February 14, 1894. At a youthful age, the boy was given two presents by his father: a violin and a monkeywrench. The violin was for if he had talent; the monkeywrench for if he had not. The violin proved more useful and Benny played the vaudeville circuit for several years, beginning at the age of seventeen. When the First World War broke out, he enlisted in the Navy, where he was put in the *Great Lakes Naval Revue,* a stage presentation for the Navy relief fund for widows and orphans. It was in this show that he found out his humorous asides got more audience response than his musical selections. He left the Navy with the mature knowledge that it was time to stop fiddling around, and to speak up for what he wanted out of life.

Even so, Benny retained the violin as a prop for his gag monologues. But now he found there was another joking violinist around, Ben Bernie. Benny Kubelsky had been calling himself Ben K. Benny. To eliminate confusion, he became Jack Benny.

Vaudeville led to Shubert musicals and *Earl Carroll's Vanities* on Broadway. A road show took Jack Benny to Hollywood, where he was spotted and put in a movie even before he began his radio work. The film was *Hollywood Revue of 1929* ("All Talking! All Singing! All Dancing!") and a couple of other features followed.

That first radio appearance where he inquired "Jack Benny . . . Who cares?" came in 1931. He was a guest on a show run by Ed Sullivan. It seems incredible to somebody of this writer's generation that the Ed Sullivan so identified with television actually preceded Jack Benny in radio, but yes, it was and yes, he did. At that time, however, The Great Stone Face was not hosting a variety show; he was reporting news and gossip as a columnist for a New York newspaper —a direct rival of the famed Walter Winchell. As part of his show, Sullivan interviewed a celebrity. Jack Benny's charm, needless to say, came across very well on radio.

Sponsors came after Benny, and they got him. He worked briefly for Canada Dry, Chevrolet, and General Tire, but his association with Jell-O desserts is the classic one. Many a middle-aged former radio listener in a jocular mood will breeze in with "Jell-O again"—Benny's greeting on the show. Though dated, it still survives as a minor part of the language.

The identification with his sponsor's product was so deep that listeners would inadvertently go into a grocery store and ask for a box of strawberry Benny. That was typical of the relationship between radio programs, their sponsors, and their listeners. Is there anyone over thirty in the United States who does not remember Jell-O when he sees Jack Benny, or think of Johnson's Wax when someone mentions Fibber McGee and Molly? Or from the other side, can you walk down cereal row in a supermarket and not think of Jack Armstrong when you see Wheaties, Tom Mix when you see a checkerboard-design box of some Ralston product, or, for at least my generation, the Lone Ranger when you see Cheerios? (Unfortunately, the special appeal of such sponsor-identification is denied today's television viewers. The economics of the industry rarely permits single sponsoring of a given show on a continuing basis. Today's advertisers are more interested in selling products through random spot commercials than in winning the loyalty of a group through sponsor-identification with one character.)

One of the things Jack Benny always insisted on in radio was that the middle commercial be a comedy one. A comic mood is hard enough to sustain without it being broken by a hard-sell pitch. So big, fat Don Wilson would lumber out to sell a big, fat bowl of Jell-O to the audience. No matter what the action might be, Don Wilson showed up at the appropriate mid-way point.

JACK: Oh, hello, Don. I didn't expect to see you here in Chinatown, in this dark alley, in the middle of a Tong war.

DON: Oh, I was just out for a stroll, and I just thought I'd drop in here at the Red Hatchet and have some Chop Suey, Sweet and Sour Pork, bamboo shoots and rice. . . .

JACK: Anything else?

DON: Why, yes, Jack, a heaping bowl of Jell-O—that tops off *any* meal . . .

JACK: I *knew* it.

DON: Jell-O, you know, Jack, comes in six delicious flavors . . .

The commercial was only one of the running gags on the *Jack Benny Show*. The jokes were repeated so often that the public began to accept them as facts. The personality of some comedians was so inconsistent that the listener never knew what to expect. In the somewhat black humor—at least, tattletale gray humor—of, say, a Henry Morgan, the comic when asked for help across the street by a little old lady, might either help her, make an amorous pass at her, or shove her under the wheels of a passing truck. If Jack Benny were asked for help across the street by the same little old lady, you *knew* there could be only one possible response: "For how much?"

It was assumed by the public that Jack Benny *was*, in fact, stingy—so much so that he allegedly had trouble getting good service in a restaurant, the waiters expecting the tiniest of tips from him. But that was show biz. Benny and his cast never tried actively to dispel the many illusions the public had about them.

"If the Boss suddenly turned generous overnight, we would all be out of business!" Rochester once observed. "When a fan asks whether Mr. Benny ever collects anything like coins, or stamps, or first editions, I always tell them he is happy to keep on collecting *money*."

Frequently, there would be fan letters demanding whether it was so that Dennis Day was paid only twelve dollars a week for singing on the coast-to-coast show, and if he actually did have to cut the grass at Mr. Benny's home as part of his contract. Naturally, the tenor earned enough to have a fine home of his own, and to hire a gardener for the lawn.

Jack Benny did not really wear a toupée or a full set of false teeth—but he *did* own a real Maxwell automobile—a 1924 model. On occasion, he drove it around Hollywood and parked it in the Brown Derby parking lot, among the Cadillacs and the Rolls-Royces. It made quite an impression, and that was what it was for. Benny did not go so far as to actually buy a live polar bear—like the one named Carmichael he kept on the show to discourage burglars. One was rented for several of his later Hollywood movies, however.

Another bit of protection from thieves—strictly on the radio show, of course—was the vault Benny had in his basement. That was where he kept all the money he never spent. Or almost never. Occasionally, on some holiday, he would be tricked into standing the whole cast to a dinner out, and so he would have to go down to the vault to take out two or three dollars. After a seemingly endless series of footsteps down a stairway and along an echoing tunnel, Jack would come upon his guard, who had been down there defending Benny's money for a long, long time. "Halt," Ed, the guard, would order. "Who goes there—Redcoat or Bluecoat?"

Ed would then try to get filled in on the latest happenings in the world above.

ED: Who's President now, Mr. Benny?
JACK: Roosevelt.
ED: Who?
JACK: Oh, I don't mean *Teddy* Roosevelt, Ed.
ED: Teddy who?
JACK: My, you have been down here a long time, haven't you?

Finally, when Benny did work the combination on the safe and swing the door open, the alarm sounded a bit like a combination of the openings of *Gangbusters* and *The Lone Ranger*.

Another mythical bit about Jack Benny's house was its location, supposedly next to the home of Mr. and Mrs. Ronald Colman. The cultured Ronnie and Benita were frequent guests on the Benny show, and could be heard complaining about Jack coming over one day and borrowing a cup and returning the next day requesting that it be filled with sugar. They tolerated Jack's boorish behavior with good humor. Jack, as usual, missed the point; he was sure they regarded him as their dearest friend.

One evening, they were serving Napoleonic brandy to their guests in exquisite seventeenth-century glasses, the last remaining set of six in the world. Jack barged in and was a bit grudgingly served a drink. A few evenings before, Jack had seen an old Ronald Colman movie, and so he knew what the very best people did after they drank a toast. Jack turned and hurled his empty glass into the embers of the fireplace.

Ronnie and Benita stood stunned, holding their antique glasses clutched to their bosoms. But the Colmans were much too cultured to embarrass even an uninvited guest by letting him think he had done the wrong thing. They, too, hurled their precious glasses into the fireplace.

Later, the Colmans could be heard discussing the evening in the bedroom of their Beverly Hills mansion. "Benita, if that man so much as steps a foot into this house again, we shall move to Pasadena!" Benny's show included many such local references, and at times the listener might be offended by the automatic, conditioned howls of the studio audience. But more often than not, he found himself joining in the laughter—for no apparent reason—at Jack's frequent references to the Le Brea tar pits or Cucamonga. Such was the power of radio.

The misunderstandings between Jack and the Colmans were mild compared to the legendary feud between Benny and Fred Allen.

On the air, Fred Allen would insinuate nasally, "Jack has no more hair than an elbow. His false teeth are so loose, they are always clicking. He is so anemic that if he stays out at night he has to get a transfusion so his eyes will be bloodshot in the morning. Before shoes were invented, Benny was a heel."

In one sketch on the *Jack Benny Show*, Fred Allen tried to take Benny's job away from him by talking to Benny's sponsor, Mr. Hill, who supposedly represented the show's new client, Lucky Strike cigarettes.

ALLEN: Well, first of all, I don't want you to think that I have anything against Benny personally . . . I'm very fond of Jack; he's one of my best friends. It's just that I hate to see him go back on the air and be a flop.

HILL: But what makes you think Benny will be a flop? He always gets laughs.

ALLEN: Mr. Hill, anyone can get laughs who tells a joke and wiggles his ears at the same time.

HILL: I'm a businessman. I don't care how a comedian gets his laughs as long as he sells the product. And I think lots of people will sit by the radio, smoke a cigarette, and listen to Jack Benny.

ALLEN: Mr. Hill, that is an impossibility . . . Smoke a cigarette and listen to Benny? How in the world can anyone smoke and hold his nose at the same time? It can't be done.

HILL: . . . When I hired Jack, I thought he had a large following.

ALLEN: He just looks that way when he's not wearing his girdle. That large following is Benny.

HILL: Do you think I could help the program if I got rid of Benny?

ALLEN: Oh, no, no . . . Just cut his part down a little . . . I think he can easily handle the tobacco auctioneer's chant.

Fred Allen's helpful, friendly visit to Jack Benny's sponsor was interrupted by a visit from Jack himself. Fred stepped into a rear office. The sponsor greeted Jack and Mary Livingstone remarking on the recent visit by Jack's old friend, Fred Allen.

HILL: Well, Jack, he said—
BENNY: That's a lie!
HILL: Now, Jack, that's no attitude to take . . .
BENNY: How can anyone like a guy who looks like he does?
MARY: Oh, Jack, Allen isn't so ugly.
JACK: How would you know? You can't see his face until you lift the bags under his eyes. And with that pained expression, he looks like a hen trying to lay a square egg . . .

However, Fred was waiting in the adjoining office, and chose a good point to re-enter. Fred and Jack exchanged a few syrupy pleasantries before they got down to business.

BENNY: Tell me, Freddy boy, what are you doing here in Hollywood?
ALLEN: Making a picture. I'm over at United Artists.
BENNY: Oh, yes, yes. I heard that Boris Karloff isn't there any more.
ALLEN: Yes, yes, and I heard that since you've been with Warner's, the *studio* isn't there any more . . .
BENNY: That settles it, Allen . . . I'd punch you right in the nose if there wasn't a lady present.
MARY: I'll leave, Jack.
BENNY: *You sit down!*

The feud was another fortunate "accident" for Jack Benny. Benny had had a child prodigy play a selection called "The Bee" on his show, and had tried to match the performance of the twelve-year-old on his own violin, proving, of course, a laughable failure. Fred Allen commented on Benny's ineptness on his own program. Benny appeared on Allen's show the following week and tried to prove he could play the violin as well as a child. He didn't make it, and Allen told him so. Thus, a "feud" was born.

Jack Benny never improved much on his violin during his radio years, even though he had regular instruction from the Frenchman, Professor LeBlanc (played by the brilliant Mel Blanc, who not only did many of the supporting characters on the show but the *sounds* as well—from Jack's insult-squawking parrot to the wheezing croak of the Maxwell's engine). During one practice session, LeBlanc kept interrupting Benny's playing by calling for "Resin!" for the strings. Again and again, "Resin! Resin!" Finally, LeBlanc demanded "Razor blade!" Jack asked what the violin instructor wanted with a razor blade. "I wish to cut my wrists," LeBlanc confided gloomily.

Perhaps the only thing worse than Jack Benny's violin playing was the singing of his close friend, George Burns. *No one* could stand Benny's fiddling, but there was at least one person who thought George Burns was the greatest singer in the world—his wife, the giddy comedienne, Gracie Allen. Burns and Allen were frequent guests on the *Jack Benny Show* and he returned the visits on their show. The topic most discussed was George's singing, and Gracie's attempts to get Jack to let George appear on the show to sing a song, or for Jack to fire Dennis Day and hire George as the permanent boy-singer on the show. Burns's vocal style was —and is to this day—unique, consisting of old vaudeville numbers reeled off at breakneck speed and in a near monotone: "*Shineonshineonharvestmoonwayupintheskiiii . . .*"

While getting ready to go on Jack's show, George and

Gracie discussed his unique singing abilities. He was un-usually modest.

GEORGE: I'll do all my singing in the bathroom—my voice belongs in the tub.

GRACIE: Your voice belongs in the Bowl . . .

GEORGE: What?

GRACIE: Thousands of women would jam Hollywood Bowl to listen to you. Ordinary crooners make bobby sox quiver, but you shake women in their foundations.

GEORGE: Honey, Hollywood Bowl is for classical singers like Nelson Eddy.

GRACIE: Oh, you're much more convincing than Nelson Eddy. When you sing "Shortin' Bread," you can actually smell it . . . Really, George . . . you're the greatest singer who ever lived.

GEORGE: Oh, not greater than Al Jolson . . .

GRACIE: Oh, poo—you are greater than Al Jolson and Frank Sinatra put together . . . What would you have if you put them together? Just a man down on his knees without the strength to get up . . . Open up the furnace of your throat and scorch me with those hot licks!

Unfortunately, the deal for George to sing on Benny's show fell through. Mary asked why, and Jack informed her: "George was willing to take the twelve dollars and fifty cents I pay Dennis Day, but after living with Gracie for twenty years, he didn't have the strength to mow my lawn." Benny was the master of the playback joke. The audience's familiarity with the reference doubled the laughter.

Jack had a lot of "trouble" with the singers on his show—the regular Dennis Day and his singing bandleader Phil Harris. Both the naïve tenor and the hard-drinking Southerner were such major talents in their own right that they ul-timately had shows of their own (Harris was joined by his wife Alice Faye) although they continued to appear on the Benny program.

There were a number of other semi-regulars on the show —the elfin Mr. Kitzel, who sold hot dogs with the "Pickle in the Middle and the Mustard on Top" (actor Artie Auerbach); the race track tout who always tried to tout Benny off on *anything*—even a flavor of Life Savers (played by the now successful television producer Sheldon Leonard); the obnoxious department store floorwalker who cried "Yeeees!" (Frank Nelson); the telephone operators, Mabel and Gertrude (Sara Berner and Bea Benadaret); and Andy Devine, who always cracked "Hiya, Buck!" and who led Jack into one of his "Buck Benny" Western skits.

When all this marvelous cast was put together, with perhaps a guest star, the *Jack Benny Show* fused into the most popular, highest-rated comedy show in broadcasting history.

PHIL: You know, Jackson, I can't understand any studio wanting to make a picture of your life.

JACK: What do you mean?

PHIL: I'm the guy. Color, glamour, excitement! That's what they should make. "The Life of Phil Harris . . ."

JACK: Phil, the story of your life wouldn't pass the Hays Office. So don't be ridiculous . . . My life has been one adventure after another. It started when I ran away from home to face the world all by myself.

PHIL: How old were you?

MARY: Thirty-two.

JACK: I was twenty-seven. I remember because I didn't want to leave until I finished high school . . . After that . . . Broadway, vaudeville, musical comedy, radio! Why, when they make the picture of my life it will be as long as *Gone With the Wind*.

MARY: It should be, they both started in the same period . . .

JACK: Well, fellows, I have to leave you now. Rochester is waiting in the car to take me to Warner Brothers . . .

(*Musical bridge*)

JACK: Take it easy, Rochester. Watch where you're going.

MARY: Oh, Jack, don't be so nervous.

JACK: I'm not nervous.

ROCHESTER: You must be, boss. You're tellin' me to take it easy, and you're drivin' . . .

JACK: Let's put the top down so people can see me.

MARY: So people can see you! Oh, Jack!

ROCHESTER: That's nothin', Miss Livingstone. This morning he wanted to ride down Hollywood Boulevard on a white horse like Lady Godiva . . . But his toupée wasn't long enough.

Hollywood has never actually filmed the life story of Jack Benny outside of this sketch, but it would make a good film, and of course the eternally thirty-nine-year-old could portray himself.

Aside from his age, there have been a lot of changes for Jack Benny. At various times there were other orchestra leaders on his show besides Phil Harris—George Olsen, Ted Weems, Frank Black, Don Bestor, Johnny Green, and finally replacing Harris, Bob Crosby. The tenor on the show changed as well—Frank Parker, Michael Bartlett, Kenny Baker, and replacing Day temporarily for his wartime service, Larry Stevens. Most of the writers remained the same for Benny as they do today in television. At one time or another, that writing staff has included Sam Perrin, Milt Josefsberg, George Balzer, John Tackaberry, Bill Morrow, Ed Beloin, and Jack Douglas. Benny, himself, attributes much of his continuing success to his association with long time producer, Irving Fein.

Jack Benny is happy to be active in television, content to be in his seventies these days. (He offers the well-known quote in expressing his attitude about his present age: "When I think of the alternative, I like it.") He feels he gets as big laughs in television as radio. In his view, he has never gotten a bigger laugh anywhere than on a television show when he picked up his folded trousers, jingled the change-laden pockets up and down and announced: "There's a quarter missing!"

The biggest laugh he ever got in *radio*, at least, is well known. Coming home late one night, he was accosted by a robber. "Your money or your life," the crook snarled. The laughter of the audience mounted higher and higher during long minutes of silence in which Jack Benny thought over that perplexing problem.

It seems appropriate that the best-loved comedian of the golden years of radio achieved his biggest laugh through silence. The laughter created by Jack Benny and all the other great radio comedians lies forever in the silence of yesteryear, but the echoes of that laughter are with some of us yet today.

13.

Down Allen's Alley

"Somebody, ah say, *somebody's* knockin' on mah door," the most famous resident of that curious sidestreet of Radioland, Allen's Alley, observed in answer to the rapping at his shanty portal.

"Yes, Senator Claghorn," Fred Allen would respond with typical nasal amiability as the door banged open, "it is I."

"Oh, it's you, son—that non-resident of mah state," said the Senator with somewhat less enthusiasm.

"Yes, I am here in my full non-voter status," Allen replied. "I hope I'm not intruding. I see you must be expecting company. You have an alligator barbecuing in the front yard."

"Always have time for anyone who might become a registered voter. Son, I see you have a question brewing—if Ah may use the expression—brewing in your mind."

"Yes, Senator Claghorn—I have the Question of the Week. 'What modern invention do you most dislike?'"

"Money," Claghorn snapped. "We in the South have very little to do with it. We believe in the barter system. For instance, if I have a chicken a fellow wants from me, he could offer to shoe mah mule for me."

"I suppose, Senator," Allen mused, "if I wanted one of your pullets I could pull off a few jokes for you."

"Son, we were talking about chickens—not eggs!"

Slam! went the Senator's door.

"The senator seems out of sorts," Allen observed for the radio audience. "His cotton gin must have jammed up on him."

The good Senator and the other residents of Allen's Alley often seemed to overshadow their creator, Fred Allen. Although Allen was one of the most creative funnymen in radio (*the* most creative in the opinion of many critics) his own fame as a comedian—a stand-up comic delivering a monologue—was somewhat eclipsed when he introduced the sidestreet peopled by notable eccentrics. Since 1932, Allen had been doing a comedy-variety show full of jokes and various sketches, but in 1943 he introduced the opening routine of Allen's Alley. Wartime censorship made freewheeling parodies of the national scene too touchy to get many past the censors. He filled one-third of the show with continuing characters, and it was through this regular cast that the *Fred Allen Show* won its greatest success.

Somewhere during his weekly interview by Fred Allen, Senator Claghorn would usually deliver one of his famous witticisms about a fellow senator. "They're going to bring Senator Aiken back . . . achin' back—haw!" And then the inevitable explanation: *"That's a joke, Son!"*

The man behind Claghorn's drawl—surely the quickest,

most enthusiastic Southern drawl in Creation—was Kenny
Delmar who left the South in his mouth behind the Mason-
Dixon line as the *Allen Show's* announcer. His fictional
solon became so popular that Delmar branched out into a
radio show all his own and made a Hollywood movie called
appropriately, *That's a Joke, Son*. As late as 1963, Senator
Claghorn had a five-minute radio show on ABC, and Delmar
is at this writing still playing the role in radio and TV commercials. There seem to be infinite possibilities in the public
official who can be ridiculed with impunity.

Senator Claghorn was a caricature of the Southern colonel
or legislator and reflected a little of the crudity of some and
the shrewdness of others in the power structure of the South.
Exaggerations led to easy visualizations for the listening audience. Though they sometimes got at the truth in ways
more realistic characters could not, the audience was not
supposed to think all United States Senators were like Claghorn, or that all Jewish housewives spoke the exotic dialect
of Mrs. Nussbaum.

"Again I am to be prodded by your poll?" Mrs. Nussbaum
would inquire at one of Allen's weekly visits to solicit her
views. The comparison of her speech patterns to those of
Molly of *The Goldbergs* is inescapable. But aside from the
accent, Mrs. Nussbaum was not a great deal different than
the canny old broads of radio like Ma Perkins or Aunt Jenny,
or one of our own aunts just up the street.

"You were expecting the Fink Spots?" Mrs. Pansy Nussbaum would ask, opening her door at Allen's knock.

"Not at all," Allen replied. "They would outweigh you by
two to one at least, Mrs. Nussbaum."

"To be sure."

"I have, Mrs. Nussbaum, for you the Question of the
Week."

"So?"

"What," asked Allen, "is the modern invention you most dislike?"

"Well . . ." Mrs. Nussbaum pondered, "well . . . present company excluded . . ."

"Thank you."

"Excluding present company, I would venture I most dislike the telephone."

"The telephone!" Allen gasped. "That is remarkable."

"I am remarking that it is remarkable." Mrs. Nussbaum went on to tell a pretty straightforward story, devoid of gag lines, of how a telephone call had interrupted her cooking procedures. In a fit of pique, Mrs. Nussbaum had thrown her telephone out the window as far as the wire would let it go.

"Then I am hearing from the patio beneath the window, 'Sorry, your time is up on the *Pot O' Gold* twenty-five thousand dollar question.' Ay-yi-yii."

"That does seem a good reason to hate the telephone," Allen agreed.

"Yes. Most of all I hate the telephone because it is always ringing while I have my head in the oven cooking."

Minerva Pious portrayed Mrs. Nussbaum and her character like that of Senator Claghorn has appeared in recent radio commercials. (Commercials today offer virtually the only employment in radio for drama and comedy performers, sound effects men, and others from the days of major network radio.) Miss Pious belongs to the small army of Jews who practice the art of comedy, one of a race that has traditionally had to accept and employ self-parody to survive. Fred Allen himself belonged to another such one-time persecuted minority, the Irish-Catholics. The character he created for Minerva Pious had less of the *schmaltz* and charm of Gertrude Berg's Molly Goldberg and more of Allen's own sometimes acid wit.

The next resident of the Alley also displayed a good deal of bite in his humor. He was the typical crusty New Englander.

"Howdy, Bub," Titus Moody responded to Allen's knock with some degree of geniality.

"Good evening, Mr. Moody. I see you must be celebrating," Allen observed. "You have the doorway strung with crab shells."

"E-yup. It's my anniversary. Married forty-one years ago terday."

"That is remarkable. How did you and Mrs. Moody meet?"

"Forty years ago and one week, I saw this young thing climbing down from a buggy . . ."

"Yes," Allen urged the old codger on.

"I attempted to help her get out of the buggy. In the process, the hem of her skirt lifted. I saw her ankle."

"And?"

"Did the decent thing. I married her."

"Mr. Moody," Allen continued, "I hate to intrude on this festive occasion, but I wonder if I might ask you the Question of the Week?"

"For thirty-nine weeks out of every year," Moody pointed out, "you ask me the Question of the Week."

"True enough," Allen admitted. "In that case, Mr. Moody, I wonder if you would tell me what modern invention you most dislike?"

"Why, that would be the radio," Moody said. "I don't hold with furniture that talks."

Fred Allen paused tellingly over this classic comment. "Perchance, do you have a more specific reason for disliking radio?"

"Put one in my henhouse to sooth the chickens."

"I see," Allen said. "Soothing music by Guy Lombardo and Sammy Kaye."

"Should have been, but by accident the radio got tuned to another station. My hens might about died from exhaustion."

"The music was too lively? Rumbas by Cugat perhaps?"

"Not that," Moody said sorrowfully. "Hens were listening to *Double or Nothing.*"

Parker Fennelly played Titus Moody, a character like the others in Allen's Alley that proved to have staying power. He is still playing the same old New Englander in commercials for Pepperidge Farm bakery products. Fennelly had played much the same old codger under other character names in such programs as *Snow Village Sketches*, predating the Allen show, but it was as Titus Moody that he found the perfect distillation of the archetypical New Englander. In writing many of the lines for Titus Moody, Fred Allen projected one aspect of his own personality. Allen had been born in Cambridge, Massachusetts, and Titus's accent was only an exaggeration of Allen's own speech pattern.

Titus Moody, Mrs. Nussbaum, and Senator Claghorn were the permanent residents and leading citizens of Allen's Alley, but there were other temporary renters from time to time. From his own Irish heritage, Allen presented the stereotyped Irish drunk in Ajax Cassidy (portrayed by master dialectician Peter Donald).

There was Falstaff Openshaw, a poet given to composing such verses as "Take Your Feet off the Table, Mother, or You'll get a Sock in the Mush." Falstaff was played by Alan Reed, today the voice of television's Fred Flintstone.

Charles Cantor played Socrates Mulligan, a most un-Socrates-like character. Later, Cantor moved to Ed "Archie"

Gardner's *Duffy's Tavern,* where he contributed perhaps the show's most popular character, the dull-witted Finnegan. "Finnegan," Archie would say, "youse is not graced wid the brains of a cockroach . . ." "*Duhhhh,* chee, t'anks, Arch!" would be the inevitable reply.*

One of the privileges of genius is nonconformity and one of the nonconformist elements in Fred Allen's make-up was his refusal to finish his radio program in exactly the twenty-nine minutes and thirty seconds allotted to him. He would not step on a line, kill a laugh, ruin a gag, just to get off the air on the dot. Today he would simply be cut off in mid-sentence and a deodorant commercial put on. In the decadent days of vintage radio, the network and the stations were loath to ruin the entertainment just to get in all the station break commercials. The Allen show frequently ran over its time period by forty-five seconds, and at times two or three minutes. (The policy of letting a program find its natural length within a reasonable fluctuation is still followed by the British Broadcasting Corporation in radio and television.)

Fortunately, the program following Allen was an audience participation show whose time span was also flexible. The program, *Take It or Leave It,* offered as its greatest challenge,

---

* Ed Gardner went from a career of writing material for comedians to becoming one himself. In 1941, he opened for the first time that fabulous saloon, *Duffy's Tavern,* saying over the phone what became the show's standard opening: "Duffy's Tavern, where the elite meet to eat. Archie, the manager speaking. Duffy ain't here. Oh, hello, Duffy . . ." We never did hear Duffy speak but could sense his frustration from Archie's opaque remarks as he described what was going on at the place—usually small disasters that Archie appeared totally unaware of. Duffy did eventually send around a management representative, his daughter Miss Duffy. "*Miss* Duffy," she would always emphasize on being introduced. The part was originally played by Shirley Booth, who went on to greater things.

the Sixty-Four Dollar Question (a prize television would increase a thousandfold). The master of ceremonies was comedian-accordionist Phil Baker who was understandably unhappy about Allen borrowing part of his, Baker's, time.

Baker began to take accurate accounting of just how much time Allen had stolen from his show. When mid-way through the season, the amount of stolen time at last added up to fifteen minutes, Baker barged into Allen's studio and began his quiz show in the middle of the *Fred Allen Show.* "Good evening, Ladies and Gentlemen," Baker shouted, "it's time to play *Take It or Leave It* with the famous *Sixty-Four Dollar Question—*" Allen stormed with simulated anger, "I'll write Senator Claghorn about this!"

It may have been prearranged, but somehow it was all part of the spontaneous excitement of which radio was capable.

Phil Baker did not offer Fred Allen the only problems he had with contest programs.

In 1934, when Major Bowes' *Amateur Hour* was at the height of its popularity, Allen was saddled by some inspired vice-president with an amateur segment as part of his variety show, *Town Hall Tonight.* Allen bore up under this incredible indignity to his talent. When one young amateur forgot to undo the safety strap that kept his accordion bellows closed as he launched into a weedily thin rendition of "Twelfth Street Rag," Allen drawled, "Son, you better unfasten that strap, or you won't get past Fourth Street."

Much later, in 1949, Fred Allen was temporarily defeated in the ratings by the giant money-paying quiz, *Stop the Music.* The great American public was offered the opportunity of choosing between one of the greatest comedians of all time and a minuscule chance at getting a telephone call offering them a shot at a pile of money. The faintest scent of fortune drowned the laughter for the majority, although a large and significant minority did chose Fred Allen.

Unlike the sponsors and networks of his day, and of ours, Fred Allen did not believe in letting polls establish public taste. He had a constant running battle with the corporate mentality; in his opinion, vice-presidents of NBC, vice-presidents of advertising agencies—in fact, *all* vice-presidents did their best to ruin his show. He made his point in a 1942 sketch. It was typically Allen and no doubt resulted in another meeting (one of many) being called—probably on the very next day—by the much-harried people he was attacking.

In the sketch, Allen, a brave man, was willing to make himself the heavy of the piece. He played the head of an advertising agency.

ALLEN: Yes, these are radio popularity ratings . . . I'm checking our agency programs. Hmm. "Fake It or Believe It" up one point two. "One Man's Relatives" up two point six . . . The —Gad! . . . Our comedy program, the "Kenny Dank Funfest" has gone down again. This is second month in succession.

MISS YUCK: What is the rating?

ALLEN: Minus two point two. That means that not only every radio listener in America isn't listening to Kenny Dank—two hundred thousand people who haven't got radios aren't listening either.

YUCK: But how can people without radios not listen?

ALLEN: One doesn't question statistics, Miss Yuck. The entire advertising business is founded on surveys. The first man who questions a survey will topple the advertising game like a house of cards . . .

YUCK: Kenny Dank is outside now.

ALLEN: Send him in here.

DANK: Hello, B.B. old sock. Ha, Ha!

ALLEN: Stop laughing at yourself, Dank. Everyone else has . . . When a comedian slips, the advertising agency has to step in.

DANK: But the last time the agency stepped in, I went down nineteen points.

ALLEN: No heresy, Dank . . . Miss Yuck, sound the conference bell.

(*The vice-presidents march in.*)

Men, we've got to change Dank's set-up.

Chorus: Check!

ALLEN: Gad, this conference is going like clockwork. Let's mother-hen that thought. We've got to hatch an idea. Let's mull, men . . .

JUMBLE: How about cutting out the actors and putting in audience participation?

DANK: You cut that out at the last conference.

FUMBLE: How about cutting out the audience and putting in actor participation?

ALLEN: You can't cut out studio audiences and render thousands of people homeless.

Fred Allen was born May 31, 1894. His mother died when he was four, and his father's sister, Elizabeth, became his second mother. The father of the man who would be known as Fred Allen was a Boston bookbinder, James Henry Sullivan. Sullivan did not make much money, but he was a jovial, fun-loving man. "I like to think I inherited Dad's wit," Allen often said. "Of course, I may only be fifty per cent correct . . ."

While he was attending the Boston High School of Commerce, which was designed to turn "Irish clods into useful bricks of industry," Fred took a part-time job in the Public Library's basement stacks. He read the books and he juggled them. Literally. One book was on the art of juggling, and he practiced with the book itself and its companion volumes.

Young Fred finally decided he was good enough to try his juggling act out in a vaudeville amateur night show. The crowd on such nights was always full of vocal critics. Catcalls and rotten eggs were routine. Occasionally, a performer would be pulled from the stage and slugged cold. Allen christened the theater the Pandemonium.

Fred Allen had been better in the library basement than he was on stage. "That was a mighty swell trick, folks. You should have been here last night when I made it." His patter was lost on the audience drunk with power at the very least.

The only person to save the Christian from the lions was Sol Cohen, a former circus strong man and then a theatrical booking agent. He took Fred under his very strong wing, telling him he had the makings of a *professional* amateur. Allen recalled that Cohen's first advice was "Louder up you got to talk!" Shades of Mrs. Nussbaum!

Fred Allen learned to talk louder and juggle faster. He won round after round of the amateur shows set up by Cohen, finally graduating to the big time, professional vaudeville in New York City. At the conclusion of his act, the stage darkened and a "magic lantern" projected images on a screen of Abraham Lincoln, Teddy Roosevelt and his Rough Riders, and finally a tattered Old Glory still waving valiantly in the breeze, all while the pit band played patriotic marches. Fred Allen was assured of getting a good hand at the end of his act.

At various times in his career, Fred Allen had been known as Young Sullivan, Paul Huckle, and Freddy James. Finally, Allen's new agent, Edgar Allen, suggested "Freddy James" take his last name. Thus, finally, Fred Sullivan became Fred Allen.

Under his new name, Fred Allen appeared in the lavish Shubert musical production, *The Passing Show of 1922*. The critics' praise established him as a comedian of importance.

The show was also important to him in that it introduced him to a pretty dancer named Portland Hoffa. "That," said Allen, "is a ridiculous name." Portland replied, "You should meet my sisters, Lebanon, Period, and Lastone."

Naturally, the two of them got married.

Fred and Portland went into radio in 1932, and stayed there.

Portland Hoffa became Allen's foil, playing opposite him on the air in much the same fashion as Gracie Allen and her comedian husband, George Burns. There was not the "cuteness" and charm of Miss Allen in Portland Hoffa's portrayal, but her denseness was as disarmingly dry as Fred Allen's wit.

PORTLAND: Hello, Mr. Allen.

ALLEN: Well, as the schoolteacher said to the little boy who spelled snow with an "E," what's snew?

PORTLAND: This is no place for jokes, Mr. Allen . . . Comedy programs today all go in for romance . . . Look at Mr. Benny. He's always taking girls out.

ALLEN: Benny with the light brown toupée? The only thing Benny ever takes out on a moonlit night is his upper plate. What gave you this romance idea, anyway?

PORTLAND: Well tomorrow is the first day of spring . . . If somebody would take out a girl we'd have something romantic to talk about . . . I know just the girl . . .

ALLEN: Who?

PORTLAND: Olive Fagelson.

ALLEN: Olive Fagelson?

PORTLAND: She'd be crazy about you. She's nearsighted.

ALLEN: Look, Portland . . . The last girl I took out left town and became a nurse with the Confederate Army.

Radio was the perfect medium for Fred Allen and perhaps the only one: his skill lay in the use of *words*. Allen could put his words in the scripts he largely wrote himself (or rather *printed* by hand), and he could pull words out of the air for any occasion. Jack Benny? "Benny couldn't *ad lib* a belch at a Hungarian banquet . . ." If some joke from the script did not go over, perhaps gaining only one guffaw from a member of the audience, Allen would remark with seeming imperturbability, "As that one lone laugh goes ricocheting around the studio, we move to a selection by Al Goodman and his orchestra . . ."

Another time he was cornered by a gushing lady who told him she had come all the way to New York from San Francisco just to see his broadcast. "Madame," intoned Allen, "if I had only known you were coming all that way just to catch my little old show, the least I could have done was meet you halfway. Say, about Omaha."

Yet Fred Allen could be generous to friends and strangers who really needed help. He had a long list of old show business people he kept on "pension" and pocketfuls of five-dollar bills to pass out to those asking for handouts.

It certainly was not a handout but a gesture of generosity to Allen when members of his old radio cast and his old nemesis, Jack Benny, gathered from all points of the globe to help the then semi-retired Allen re-create his program on the television show, *Omnibus*, in 1952.

"A lot of people never realized the feud between Fred Allen and myself was a joke," Jack Benny observed. "Unfortunately, one of the people who never realized it was Fred." (That in itself was a joke, of course.)

For the last time, on that telecast of *Omnibus*, Fred Allen ventured down Allen's Alley. Due to a heart condition, he was never able to work hard enough to do a full-scale comedy-variety show on TV, which required a great deal of rehearsal. After this special *Omnibus* program, he would go on for years as a panelist on *What's My Line?*, but he would never again perform with his old cast.

For this occasion, Fred asked the Alley residents different questions culled from past shows.

He asked of Mrs. Nussbaum: "Do you think advertising affects our customs?"

NUSSBAUM: A girl I am knowing, Cuddles . . . a bouncer at the Y.W.C.A. . . . One day Cuddles is seeing advertised a perfume . . . "Capitulate" . . . It is like "Surrender," only *stronger.*
ALLEN: Gosh!
NUSSBAUM: The advertising is saying "Girls using the handy size one quart bottle is positively guaranteed a man . . ." Cuddles is not taking any chance. Cuddles is pouring on herself *two* quarts.
ALLEN: The two quarts worked?
NUSSBAUM: Cuddles is eloping with a Siamese twin.

The question for Titus Moody was "Do you have a hobby?"

MOODY: Why, I one time was collecting deer ends.
ALLEN: Deer ends?
MOODY: Everybody was collecting deer heads, so I started collecting what was left over.
ALLEN: I see.
MOODY: I had twenty deer ends mounted on the wall . . . When I opened the door, seemed like I was over-taking a herd.

Finally, Fred Allen came to a door draped in the Confederate flag and rapped on the panel with a knocker made from the handle of a cotton gin. The good Senator Claghorn appeared.

ALLEN: How are you going to spend Thanksgiving?
CLAGHORN: With my kinfolks, son. What a day . . . We start out

with a Memphis Martini . . . That's a tall glass of pure corn
likker with a wad of cotton in it . . . a Boll Weevel is riding
the cotton . . . Then comes Alligator Chowder . . . a whole
alligator simmering in swamp water . . .

ALLEN: Yum-yum! Do you have turkey with the meal?

CLAGHORN: Mock Turkey, son. That's a racoon, stuffed with grits
and Magnolia buds . . . Then we stand and give thanks . . .
Thanks for not being born in the North!

The final trip down Allen's Alley was over. Perhaps it
proved that a Jewish housewife who fixed up her friend
with a Siamese twin, a senator who believed the Civil War
had never happened, and a farmer who liked the rear ends
of animals were better heard than seen.

There was one more part, however, to the re-creation of
the radio show on television. Fred Allen's greatest character
was Fred Allen himself. He had a voice that sounded like
"a man with false teeth chewing on slate pencils," managing
to "sound like an articulate spider enticing a fly to a webbed
pratfall." But when he added to this remarkable voice a
Chinese accent, he became the greatest of all Oriental detectives, One Long Pan.

PAN: Ah, greetings and Shalom, kiddies—One Long Pan, oriental
Dick Tracy on the job.

NORBERT: I say, old boy, will you stop breaking your English on
my premises?

PAN: Who are you, little man?

NORBERT: I, Sir, am Norbert Nottingham.

PAN: Very suspicious. What you do here? . . . Long Pan formerly
M.C. *What's My Line?* You work for profit-making organiza-
tion?

NORBERT: This is ridiculous . . . Sir Cedric has shot himself—
committed suicide!

PAN: Suicide likely story. Not so fast. Long Pan look around. Long Pan examine body. Ho-ho-ho—you see—in Sir Cedric's hand?

NORBERT: What?

PAN (*pointing to gun*): A lewolerwer!

NORBERT: A lewolerwer?

PAN: A lewolerwer!

In closing that *Omnibus* telecast, Allen quoted from his book, *Treadmill to Oblivion.*

"There was a certain type of imaginative comedy that could be written for and performed only on radio," Fred Allen observed. "But we are living in a machine age, and for the first time the comedian is being compelled . . . to compete with a machine . . . Whether he knows it or not, the successful comedian is on a treadmill to oblivion."

Yet, although the name "Fred Allen" will one day only be a footnote in the history of broadcasting, it is likely that some of his wit and style will be reflected in our funny men for generations to come. That is, unless Fred Allen's prediction bears fruit absolutely and our comedians become no longer human, leaving us only a machine to laugh at. Who knows? After all, television already has a machine to do the audience's laughing for them. Will it, one day, be a world full of machines laughing at machines?

Index